DATE DUE

MY 21 '97			
SE 30 '97			
OC 21 '97			
DE 16 97			
JY 22 '09			
OC 23 '01			

DEMCO 38-296

THE QUEST FOR SELF

TAKESHI IIZUKA

The Quest for Self

Zen in Business and Life

NEW YORK UNIVERSITY PRESS
NEW YORK AND LONDON

NEW YORK UNIVERSITY PRESS
New York and London

Library of Congress Cataloging-in-Publication Data
Iizuka, Takeshi, 1918-
The quest for self : Zen in business and life / Takeshi Iizuka.
p.   cm.
Includes index.
ISBN 0-8147-3757-9 (alk. paper)
1. Religious life—Zen Buddhism.   2. Business—Religious aspects—
Zen Buddhism.   3. Businessmen—Religious life.   I. Title.
BQ9286.I39   1995
294.3'444—dc20   95-10488
                        CIP

New York University Press books are Smyth-sewn,
and printed on permanent and durable acid-free paper.

Manufactured in the United States of America

10   9   8   7   6   5   4   3   2   1

Contents

Preface   ix

1 The Original Landscape   1

Living Life   1
The Weight of Parental Love   3
Emergence from the Shell of Weakness   6
Do Not Resent the Success of Others   9
The Sutra of the Weight of Parental Kindness   11
Unenlightened and Ignorant People   14

2 The Master's Teachings   17

True Enlightenment Is Not Enlightenment, True Emptiness
   Is Not Emptiness   17
The Ultimate Way Is Not Difficult, It Simply Rejects
   Discrimination   20

Ueki Rōshi's Eyes   22
The Highest Way of Life   25
Thoroughly Purifying the Self   27
Seeking Always to Go Forward   30

3 The Fundamentals of Mind   33

Seeking the True Self   33
    What Is the True Self?   33
The Workings of Mind   35
Illusion   37
Seeking the Self   40
How to Seek the Self   42
No-Thought   44
Join Not Two Thoughts Together   47
Prevailing over the Self   49
Can the Human Character Be Changed?   52
The Conclusive Experience of Emptiness   54
Two Epistemological Views Concerning Reality   56
To Realize Emptiness Is to Have the Ability to Change Fate   58
Transcendental Consciousness   61
Keep This in Mind!   63
Choosing Your Destiny   65
    Choices that Determine a Person's Destiny   65
Ruin from a Moment's Mistaken Judgment   67
Compromise or Destruction of the Ego?   69
Why Company Employees Fail   73
Attaining True Insight   76
    Some Thoughts on Attaining Intuitive Power   76
Acquiring the Power of Insight   79
Toward Insight   82
Two Necessary Conditions for Attaining Insight   84
The Shortest Route to Attaining Insight   86
Going beyond Insight   88
Three Conditions for Living the Highest Form of Life   91
Cultivating the Mind   93

4 The Wisdom of the Buddha   97

Raise Thought without Letting It Settle on Any Particular Thing   97
Hui-neng, the Sixth Patriarch   100
The Āgamas   102
Bankei   105
The Sense of Fear   107
Meditation Training   110

Conclusion: Making the Most of the Now   113

The True Nature of Self-Interest   113
The Importance of Forging Self-Control   115
Seeing the Mountain, Not Seeing the Mountain   117
Attitudes toward Adversity   119
Kill, Kill, Kill the Self, Kill It Completely. When Nothing Is Left,
    Become a Teacher of Others   121
Benefiting Both Self and Others   123

Appendix 1   127
Appendix 2   139
Appendix 3   149
Index   161

Preface

We all know that human life is lived only once, and then only for a century or less. Because we have such a short sojourn in life, it becomes all the more important to ask how we should best live it. I have compiled in this volume a series of essays that first appeared in the TKC company monthly newsletter, *Tokoshie,* in the hopes that my own thoughts on the matter will be of help to others in approaching this vital question.

Zen Master Hakuin, the eighteenth-century priest who restored Japanese Zen, spoke of himself with humility in *Yabukōji* (Spearflower), which he wrote in commemoration of the fiftieth anniversary of his mother's death, saying, "How could such an insignificant grain of dust such as myself not become a priest?" This same kind of extreme humility was shown by Saichō, the priest who brought Tendai

Buddhism to Japan early in the ninth century. In the seventh month of 785, soon after receiving full ordination as a Buddhist priest and being accepted into the official clerical hierarchy, he suddenly left the center of power and climbed into the fastnesses of Mount Hiei, northeast of what is now Kyoto, there to undertake austere religious practice, "sitting under trees and upon stones." He composed a vow at that time, which read in part, "I, Saichō, the most foolish of fools, the most crazy of the crazy, the lowest of deluded beings, have diverged from the buddhas, have transgressed the imperial law and have been amiss in filial piety and propriety." What a remarkable depth of humility and self-criticism in one short sentence! I believe that the words of these two great priests are true reflections of their outlook. I have much to learn from them.

May 1994   Takeshi Iizuka

1

The Original Landscape

LIVING LIFE

We live our lives only once, whoever we are. When I attended funerals as a heedless youth, I felt that death was only a matter for others and had nothing to do with me.

In the spring of 1939 I was a law student at Tōhoku Imperial University (present-day Tōhoku University). I remember (though vaguely, for it was well over fifty years ago) reading a book popular among students at that time called *Einleitung in die Philosophie* (Introduction to Philosophy) by the German philosopher and leader of the Marburg school of neo-Kantianism, Wilhelm Windelband (1848–1915). In it I came across the sentences "What is life?" ("Was ist das Leben?") and "Life is but a single existence" ("Das Leben ist das Einmalige"). Those words struck me like lightning. I believe it was Kobayashi Issa (1763–1827) who wrote:

1

What I thought until now
Was to do with others—
Ah, that I too will die
I cannot bear it!

I felt exactly the same way. It is embarrassing to relate, but I was so overwhelmed by the thought that I was going to die one day, that I was never going to live but this once, that I could not sleep at all that night.

It must seem foolish getting so worked up about what is, after all, the natural course of events. Nevertheless, when I actually experienced this revelation my grief was almost unbearable. Then, at some point, a question began to burn in my mind: "If I am to live only once, how should I best live my life?" I came to realize that each moment of life must be lived to the fullest, and I made that my goal. I was influenced, too, by the words of a poem made popular by Takeko Kujō (1887–1928), an ill-fated beauty of the 1920s:

Just look!
Even the blossoms that are destined to fall tomorrow
Are blooming now with all their might.

At that time I was spending my summers at Unganji Temple in Nasu, and I had many chances to converse with the master, Giyū Ueki Rōshi. He took me aside on one instance and said to me, "Iizuka, life is passion. Those who bring passion to their pursuits gain the greatest success." Devote yourself heart and soul to everything, I thought. Right! I resolved from then on, since after all I was a student, to get through a hundred pages of original foreign-language works and two hundred pages of Japanese literature every day. If I was to do this, however, I would have no time to travel to the university and attend my courses there. Deciding that the university was a waste of time, I did not attend classes for more than a total of two weeks until I graduated. As a result only a few classmates know my face, and not a single professor remembers it.

There was a certain Professor Katsumoto who taught civil law at Tōhoku Imperial University. Naturally I appeared in his class for only a single period (about two hours), and of course the professor retained no memory of me at all from the classroom. After the war I became fairly well acquainted with him and was often in and out of his house. He once asked me, "Excuse the question, but did you really graduate from Tōhoku Imperial University?" I replied, "It's only natural that you don't remember me because I only attended your course for one period, but I can prove I did attend your lecture!" I went on to describe the double-breasted navy suit he had worn on that day and how he had put his left hand into his coat pocket and told us an anecdote about Sir William Blackstone, the great eighteenth-century legal scholar from Oxford. I related how he had spoken to us of the problem of *clausula rebus sic stantibus* (the principle of changing conditions) that had been taken up by his own law professor. Astounded, Professor Katsumoto stopped me. "You don't have to say any more. I believe you were a student at Tōhoku University!" Perhaps it was thanks to my depth of concentration in those days that I could remember so much.

THE WEIGHT OF PARENTAL LOVE

As a young child I had an extremely weak constitution. We received a medical examination at the beginning of every school year in elementary school, and it was a foregone conclusion that the school doctor would remind my class teacher that I should not be allowed to take part in the annual athletic festival. As a result I did not once participate during my six years in elementary school in an event that is a high point for every student.

I felt very sad and lonely. My father, who worked for a bedding firm, lamented unceasingly to my mother that I would not be able to succeed him. All the same he seemed to have decided to make me a strong child, for as soon as I left the hospital following an accident during my first year of school, he began getting me up at four every morning and taking me out to do physical exercise. In summer it was already light, but in winter we would go out into pitch blackness. Rain or snow, he took me out for a training session every morning for six years without a break. When I think of his love for me now, I am overwhelmed to the point of tears with gratitude and fondness. I think my father grieved that his only son was physically weak, but he never showed his grief to me, he showed only unfailing encouragement. Coaxing and humoring a son who was often recalcitrant, he took me out to exercise every day without fail.

Being a schoolchild I was unable to converse on an adult level, and my father was probably equally lonely. On the way to our training area he would often walk along awkwardly, humming Noh chants he had learned from a friend in the neighborhood. What training we did was completely without equipment, because we were too poor to buy anything. The two of us would face each other on the bank of the Kurokawa River, which flowed near our home, and shout in turn in the loudest voices we could manage. Occasionally we went to a nearby hill called Goten'yama, where there had once been a fortification, and exchanged shouts similarly on the hillside. In the fourth year of this training my father went off alone to visit his elder brother, who was living in Seoul. This brother, whose name was Tōru, was the personal physician of the Lee family, the former rulers of Korea. He also operated a prosperous dental clinic in a section of Seoul. On his return my father brought back with him a large amount of secondhand clothing and shoes that had belonged to people in the upper reaches of society. That was the summer I was in fourth grade. As a present my father bought me a football. At last we had something to use in our training! From then on we would kick and throw the ball every morning during our training period.

Without realizing it, I gradually regained my health. From around the time my father bought a football for me I fell into the habit of visiting Kōmyōji Temple, a local temple of the True Pure Land sect, between our training session and the hour I had to set off for school. During that time I would put all my effort into chanting the *Shōshinge*, a scripture written by Shinran that is chanted daily, morning and evening, by his followers, under the guidance of the priest. Looking back now at that ten-year-old sitting before the Buddhist altar with his palms held reverently before him, his mind still a blank page, I ascribe my aptitude for things religious to my father's training.

Despite my physical weakness, I was always at the top of my class, scoring full marks in every subject. When I took my report card home at the end of the term, my father would always comment happily, "Your teacher must have made a mistake!" I eventually went on to study commerce at the

Kanuma Agricultural and Commercial School. As I was starting my first term there my father told me that I would work for the famous Tokyo bedding firm, Nishikawa, after graduation. I determined then to become the best bedding craftsman in Japan, just like my father. As the time for my graduation approached, however, my history teacher came to see my father. I sat very still on the other side of the paper door and listened, curious to discover what my teacher had come to discuss. "We have never had a boy in the school with such excellent results," he said. "I hope very much that your son will be able to go on to higher education." My father offered no reply at that time, perhaps thinking it was an economic impossibility. Deploring my father's indecisiveness, I argued passionately with him. It was my mother who said to me, "Even if I have to reduce our meals from three to two, I will let you go on with school." I would not be the person I am today were it not for my father's practical demonstration of his true love for me and my mother's encouragement, born of indomitable love.

EMERGENCE FROM THE SHELL OF WEAKNESS

"I never thought they'd be able to raise you," said my old first-grade teacher, Mr. Iizuka, pouring saké into my cup at an elementary school reunion in the autumn of 1959. It was not an unreasonable statement. One summer evening in 1926, when I was in first grade, I was hit by a speeding bicycle and thrown about four meters. I was taken to Eda Hospital in Utsunomiya, where I spent the next six months. It was as a result of the accident that I was never permitted by the school doctor to take part in the annual athletic festival. I was extremely weak physically. All the same, when Mr. Iizuka recalled those events of thirty-three years before, I, then forty years old, received a considerable shock. I felt my old teacher's affection and experienced a warm glow in my chest. More than thirty years have passed since that meeting, and Mr. Iizuka is no longer in the world.

My childhood and youth were a constant complaint about my weakness and an ongoing battle against it. It was not just a matter of physical weakness. Sadly, I also lacked mental stamina. I could never stick to a study plan for more than three days. The defeatism suffered by the weak is a sad and dispiriting thing for which there is no recourse. It was when I was at my lowest that Professor Katayama of Risshō University visited my school to give a lecture. I think it was in the summer of my third year of middle school, when I was fifteen. I have completely forgotten what the professor spoke about in his lecture, but whatever it was, it made a deep impression on me. Afterwards, when we were streaming out of the hall and milling around the corridor, I caught sight of the professor over the heads of the other students, pushed my way up to him, and clutched his coat. "Professor, help me!" I cried. The professor was puzzled. "What is it?" he asked gently. Oblivious of my surroundings, I explained. "I'm weak," I said. "I can't stick to a study plan for even three days. I want more than anything to be strong. Help me!" I was sobbing by this time. "Son," said the professor, "I was just the same." What words of salvation those were! The professor told me that when he was young, he would visit a temple and cry to the priest there about exactly the same thing. The priest told him to douse himself in thirty buckets of cold water daily, as a result of which he would become strong, peeling away the layers of weakness one by one. Standing there in the corridor, the professor told me that he had done as instructed, dousing himself with thirty buckets of water a day, and that he had become much stronger mentally as a result.

I did as Professor Katayama recommended from that time until I left the university. In the freezing winters of Sendai, where my university was located, it was difficult to break the ice when the bath water froze so that I could douse myself. My strength of purpose gradually hardened, however, just as the professor had said it would, and I came to feel as if my consciousness and subconscious were always united. I had also, from the summer of my sixteenth year (1935), practiced Zen meditation under the direction of Ueki Rōshi of Unganji Temple, again in an attempt to overcome my weakness. I continued this practice for thirty-two years, until the Rōshi's death in May 1967.

I know from personal experience that when my consciousness becomes unified with my subconscious there is no longer either strength or weakness, and I am able to act as I wish. When there is no weakness, there is no strength either. This is the greatest state of relaxation a human being can attain. I realized that surprising talents and wisdom are concealed within this state. As a result of this experience, human beings can attain the six superhuman powers mentioned in the *Lotus Sutra*, even changing the course of their own destiny. Life's guides are to be found everywhere. The determining factor for human life is a purity and honesty of mind that can accept instruction with humility. I have come to realize the fallacy of Schopenhauer's assertion that a person's character is unalterable.

DO NOT RESENT THE SUCCESS OF OTHERS

In *The Analects of Confucius* is the expression, "Do not resent the success of others." During the early summer of my eighteenth year I read the *Analects* while walking along the road, and this phrase has surprisingly stuck in my mind so that even today, more than fifty years later, it comes welling up at various times. It means something like not having any feelings of revenge or antagonism toward those who overtake us or surpass us. A truly great person is like this. He or she is able to live consistently at his or her own pace.

Perhaps I should explain why I was reading the *Analects* along the road. At that time I was in my second year at the Fukushima Higher Commercial School. I had left the school's dormitories after completing my first year, as school policy dictated, and I had trouble finding suitable accommodation. My parents sent me twenty-five yen a month, which was less than the going monthly rate for accommodation and two meals a day at the time. Even if I could have used the twenty-five yen for room and board, I would have had no money for lunch or for the books and notepads I needed. Thus, I had to find someplace that charged less. Finding no place in the city of Fukushima that would take me for what I could pay, I thought of Manganji Temple, a Zen temple in a village about six kilometers from the city. It belonged to the Rinzai sect of Zen, and I had visited it once during my first year for a Zen meditation session with a Buddhist youth group headed by Professor Meijirō Sakakibara. I went off alone to the temple to plead with the resident priest, Sōen Ōkuma, for permission to board there, explaining my family's circumstances and promising to be satisfied with the simplest food. It was decided that I would live at the temple for twelve yen a month. Though there was a bus to the city from that side of the Abukuma River, I did not have enough money to take it and so walked the twelve kilometers to school and back every day. At first the walk exhausted me, and for about a month I hardly had energy to study. Once I was used to it though I began to think it was a waste of time just to walk along the road. I realized that, in terms of the theory of marginal utility I was learning at school, it probably rated zero.

I therefore decided to use my commuting time to memorize the *Analects,* thinking it could not be so very difficult to master its five hundred or so small sections. I went off to the bookstore to buy myself a copy and began memorizing it day by day as I walked to and from school. It was from the *Analects* that I extracted a large number of the teachings that were to guide me in my youth. When I came across the expression, "Do not resent the success of others," I admired the breadth of someone who could act like that and, upon examination, found myself to be quite different. Encountering my weaknesses time after time, I determined to be firm in my ideas regarding the way of life I wished to live in the future. When I returned to my parents' home in Kanuma, Ibaraki Prefecture, for the summer holidays, I tried talking with my father about Confucius's words, but I was saddened to find that I could not make him understand.

In spite of my weak constitution I had the one strength of being unyielding, and it was very difficult for me to understand how not to be antagonistic to those who surpassed me. I repeated Confucius's words over and over again to myself, and now, well over fifty years later, the phrase remains alive in my memory.

I have had some ten drivers over the years. One of them, a Mr. T., hated to let other cars pass him. He would rev up the engine just as they were about to overtake and speed ahead of them. I once counted to myself, as we drove between the house in Kanuma and my home in Chigasaki, the cars we overtook during the journey, and ended up with a total of one hundred and seventy. Mr. T.'s state of mind was astonishing, I thought. Mr. M., the driver I employed after Mr. T., was, on the contrary, wholly admirable in his job. He seemed to make a mission of his occupation. However often other cars overtook him, he remained oblivious and maintained his own pace. An unyielding person suffers greatly when overtaken during the race of life. I think it is of the greatest importance that we should be able to hold to our own pace, retaining a broad view of our lives and avoiding being sidetracked by immediate phenomena.

THE SUTRA OF THE WEIGHT OF PARENTAL KINDNESS

In the summer of 1937, when I was nineteen, a charitable benefactor distributed miniature copies of the *Sutra of the Weight of Parental Kindness* to every student in my school. I took my copy back to the temple where I was boarding and read it over and over again. There were three students living at Manganji at that time, in a detached building with three small rooms off a long narrow corridor. Tetsutarō Umeda, Morio Izawa, and I occupied one room each and vied with each other in our studies.

A wisteria vine had coiled itself over the roof of the corridor, and in the spring its lavender flowers hung in great clusters thirty or forty centimeters long. Walking along the corridor was like stepping under a floral arch, and I felt I was at play in a sweet-smelling garden. Maybe I am succumbing in my memories to what psychology calls "memory beautifying the past," but from my vantage point of close to sixty years later my school days seem like paradise. I managed on the meager sum of twenty-five yen a month; I was well satisfied with the simple temple fare of soup, rice, and one vegetable; and I delighted in my weekly manjū, a bun filled with sweet bean paste that I bought for five sen each Saturday. My school lunch was no more than a rice ball smeared with fermented bean paste and wrapped in bamboo bark, and every day I walked the same twelve kilometers to and from school. When the lunch siren sounded my schoolmates would all hurry off to the cafeteria, leaving me alone in the auditorium to gobble down my rice ball and when I had finished to quench my thirst from the tap. My peers looked at me somewhat askance as they passed by me in silence, thinking what a strange fellow I was. I was consoled and inspired, though, by a passage in the *Analects* I had read on my way to school: "There is no point in seeking the views of a gentleman who, though he sets his heart on the Way, is ashamed of poor food and poor clothes" (*The Analects of Confucius,* trans. D. C. Lau, Penguin Books, 1979). It moved me deeply, and I repeated it to myself over and over again.

The money I received each month from my parents did not, of course, drop into their laps from heaven; as my mother had said, "Even if I have to reduce our meals from three to two, I will let you go on with school," and my parents scrimped and saved out of their own difficult lives to give their son an education. The monthly board of twelve yen I paid to the temple was itself particularly low. The priest of Manganji, Sōen Ōkuma, had allowed me to stay for that amount out of his regard for Ueki Rōshi, who had been a senior of his when both were doing their Zen training as youths at Myōshinji Temple in Kyoto, and under whom I was now studying. The average rate for a room and two meals at the time was between twenty-five and twenty-seven yen; I was paying less than half that. My fellow boarders Umeda and Izawa, having learned of my arrangement, had come to me and begged me to act as intermediary for them with the priest Sōen Ōkuma to allow them to stay at the temple as boarders as well.

During my time at Manganji I went outdoors every night to do Zen meditation on the side of the hill facing the Abukuma River, which flowed in front of the temple gate. Almost fifty years later, my old companion Tetsutarō Umeda, meeting me again, remarked when I asked that he never knew I had done that.

Once I was meditating outdoors at night after a heavy snowfall. As usual, I had gone off to the hillside near the temple gate with my cushion and wooden sword. I sat down on a large tree stump and folded my legs into position to begin meditation. Suddenly, I heard a thumping noise coming from somewhere. I looked around but could see nothing but the deep snow. I surveyed the bright snow guardedly, but could discern no movement. Then I realized that what I was hearing was my own heart beating. Years later, I told Ueki Rōshi about this, but he dismissed the possibility flatly. Even he had never had that experience, it seems.

In any event, it was in the summer of my nineteenth year that I came across the *Sutra of the Weight of Parental Kindness.* My actual contact with my parents was now very limited, but I realized how much they had struggled to raise me. Standing alone in the corridor I raised a voiceless cry as I stared up at the sky over the town where I was born, and tears of gratitude poured down my cheeks.

UNENLIGHTENED AND IGNORANT PEOPLE

"Unenlightened and ignorant" is a phrase that appears in Buddhist sutras, where Śākyamuni talks about his resignation and grief at being unable to bring deliverance to those who lived in perpetual ignorance, in a state of unenlightenment and delusion.

Do we really have to discuss heavy topics such as the best way for human beings to live? Surely it is enough to be able to spend our time doing interesting and pleasant things. Some would say the problem is money—the pressing question of how to save it. Others do not care so much about money, but want instead to make a good marriage in order to have fine children. Others might prefer to put aside both money and marriage for fame. After all, did not the great nineteenth-century Japanese historian Rai San'yō write: "Oh, to have a place in history!" How good it would be to leave one's name in history, at least in Japan's modern history, if not on the world stage! Still others are different again. Remember Cervantes? He wrote one of the masterpieces of world literature, *Don Quixote,* when he was in prison. That is what is most attractive to some—to strive for a particular goal or direction in life. Yet it is an indisputable fact that for a good many people, life means no more than eating, sleeping, and, eventually, dying, and they have never striven to discover their real purpose in life.

There is a man in my accounting office I will call M. Whenever I think about him, I cannot help sighing to myself. We have worked in the same office for more than twenty years, but I am still no closer to understanding his goals in life than I was when I first met him. All I can think is that he has never attempted to probe his own essence. I am not implying that he intentionally tries to do anything bad. Nor is he by any means inferior when it comes to brains. Indeed, he graduated from one of the most prestigious universities. The problem is that though others look upon him as a man of some wisdom, he lacks something. There is a considerable gap between him and the general run of men. I conjecture that what he is now is the result of his never having forced himself to plumb the depths of his mind to discover his true, still concealed desires, of which he remains unaware. He has never pushed himself to ask exactly who he really is. I say this because he is a terrible egoist, almost to a clinical degree.

All the same, it is a difficult task for ordinary people to crush the hard shell of unconscious habits that surround the mind. Only a person who has undergone religious training at the risk of life itself can accomplish it. When it has been achieved, however, all former points of reference are destroyed, and a whole new world opens up. It is something like de Bono's "lateral thinking," in which everything vanishes like mist in a vast realm that could be called the cosmos or space. Some people would say this is worse than death itself. There is no consciousness of self within one's mind, and there is therefore, of course, no distinction between oneself and others. Attaining such a state is beyond all imagination. For six years Śākyamuni, the Buddha, led a life of utmost frugality and asceticism. His ancient biographer Asaṅga describes how, in the bone-piercing nighttime cold of the forests of northern India, Śākyamuni ate only one jujube berry, one grain of barley, and one flax berry for his meals. Of greater importance, though, is the nature of his religious practice. Śākyamuni himself provides us with the answer: "To discover who I really was" and "To find my real self." This is a quest that gives absolutely no return in monetary terms; today we would be inclined to consider someone mad who spent six years in the search for self. The true value of life cannot, however, be counted in monetary terms. Śākyamuni struggled to the very limits of his life to acquire that which is beyond price. His actions seem inexplicable to anyone who does not understand their value.

Whenever I think of M. I feel the weight of karma human beings carry with them. I have probably spent more time than the man himself trying to find a means to help him change, but I have had no success as yet. Have you ever seen someone whose karma is so heavy that it is like an immovable rock? I am convinced that we must have the experience of seriously learning during our youth at the feet of one we look upon as our life's master how we ourselves should live our lives, before our hearts harden with various preconceptions and ideas. As my life draws near its close I still consider that it was my greatest good fortune to have been tempered, between my sixteenth and forty-eighth years, by Giyū Ueki Rōshi. Without his severe training I would not have become the person I am today.

2

The Master's Teachings

TRUE ENLIGHTENMENT IS NOT ENLIGHTENMENT, TRUE EMPTINESS IS NOT EMPTINESS

The words "True enlightenment is not enlightenment; true emptiness is not emptiness" are to be found in the Zen classic, *The Transmission of the Lamp,* accounts of Chinese masters compiled in 1004. If we are conscious of having attained true and correct enlightenment we have not achieved enlightenment at all, for we are caught up in its idea rather than its reality. Similarly, even if we consider that we have achieved absolute enlightenment, this is not the true enlightenment that goes beyond all duality, what we call "emptiness."

People think Zen is a religion whose goal is enlightenment, but this "enlightenment" is something of a scoundrel. In my sixteenth summer I began to practice Zen under Giyū Ueki

17

Rōshi of Unganji Temple in Nasu, Tochigi Prefecture. At first I understood nothing and suffered dreadfully. I had begun Zen meditation thinking that all I had to do was achieve a state of "no-thought," but it was not easy to reach this state of mind. Like clouds sailing over the mountains, extraneous and delusory thoughts floated unbidden into my mind; rather than being in a state of "no-thought," my mind was like a rubbish heap. This was no good, but what was I to do? I had just started out on the endless path of religious practice. When I happened to glance at Ueki Rōshi he always seemed to be in a state of "no-thought," reacting to everything that occurred like a flash of lightning, astonishingly quickly. I admired his apparently limitless understanding. At the same time, though, the Rōshi always appeared relaxed, never restless. I thought him wonderful, but I had no idea how to attain such a state myself. In the meantime I aimed at achieving the state of "no-thought," and strove to approach it and become familiar with it. That year I was staying at Unganji for my entire summer holiday, about forty days. It goes without saying that I was deeply impressed with the life there. You can gauge how impressed I was by the fact that I remained as a student of Ueki Rōshi for the next thirty-two years.

The next summer, too, I spent at Unganji. I had graduated from the Kanuma Agricultural and Commercial School and was now a student at the Fukushima Higher Commercial School. There I had joined a Buddhist youth group run by one of our teachers, Meijirō Sakakibara. I had gone with Mr. Sakakibara to do meditation at a Zen temple called Manganji Temple on the outskirts of Fukushima, thus establishing the connection that led to my boarding there from my second year. It is strange how specific events determine life's turning points, for at the time of my first visit I had no idea that I would end up living there one day. During my first year I lived, like all boys of my age at school who did not commute from their homes, in a dormitory. I lived upstairs in the west block; I had been "volunteered" as dormitory leader for my block when I had gone to the lavatory. There were three blocks altogether, the east, central, and west; Morio Izawa and Tetsutarō Umeda, who were later to be my fellow boarders at Manganji, were in the west and central blocks, respectively. With more than a hundred vigorous and excitable teenage boys living together, a great deal of roughhousing went on. I remember once a whole room was flooded with water.

In March of the following year (1937), at the beginning of my second year, I had to leave the dormitory. In urgent need I visited Manganji and asked the priest, Sōen Ōkuma, to permit me to board at the temple. Izawa and Umeda later joined me. During the two years I lived there I practiced meditation extensively in the temple garden, on the hillside behind the temple, on the hill in front of the temple and on a cliff above the Abukuma River. You can see I was not at a loss for places to sit. I have an especially vivid recollection of meditating on the artificial hill in the large temple garden where I had the experience of having my breath almost stop, and on the hillside in front of the temple, amid deep snow, where I heard my own heart beating.

After I moved to Tōhoku Imperial University in 1939, I boarded at Kotaki Onsen, occupying the same room Lieutenant Aizawa had used. I also visited the priest Myōdō Gikan of Taibaiji Temple, mentioned by name in the Sōseki Natsume novel *Kusa makura* (The Three-Cornered World). He taught me the expression, "A mind convinced is naturally free." That is, it is important to be able to assent to the good in something and, at the same time, to have a mind as natural as the dispersing clouds and the vanishing mist. At such times the mind is perfectly clear with no obstructions; it penetrates the emptiness (void), or *śunyatā* in Sanskrit, without even conceiving of the emptiness. This is what is meant by "True enlightenment is not enlightenment, true emptiness is not emptiness."

THE ULTIMATE WAY IS NOT DIFFICULT, IT SIMPLY REJECTS DISCRIMINATION

"The ultimate Way is not difficult, it simply rejects discrimination" are the first words of a poem called "On Believing in Mind" by Master Chien-chih (d. 606), the third patriarch of Ch'an (Zen) in the lineage of Bodhidharma.

Every summer from the time I was sixteen, it was my custom to live at Unganji Temple in Nasu as a student of Ueki Rōshi. I remember that I was seventeen when I first came across Chien-chih's words. At that time Ueki Rōshi used to have all the monks and students gather daily in the main hall of the temple soon after the rest period following breakfast, and there he would lecture us on Zen scriptures. When I was sixteen it was the *Records of Lin-chi,* and the summer I was seventeen it was "On Believing in Mind." The meaning of Chien-chih's words is quite easy to understand. "The ultimate Way" for Buddhism can be understood as "enlightenment." What Chien-chih meant is that the way to enlightenment is not at all difficult. It suffices that we remain aloof from all discrimination, selectivity, and clinging. We are inclined to think of enlightenment as extremely difficult, something beyond the reach of ordinary people, but that is not so. We only need a mind free from discrimination. My first reaction on hearing this was astonishment that Zen enlightenment should be so easy.

What is the most highly regarded and important thing in life? Is it to make large amounts of money? Is it to acquire social position, by becoming a politician, a company president, a mayor, or a prefectural governor, for example? Or is it, in Rai San'yō's words, "Oh, to have a place in history for a thousand years!" Everybody worries when young about his or her true purpose and goal in life. My late school friend Izawa once said when we stayed up all night talking, "I think that the purpose of life is to find a good wife and have fine children and grandchildren." Impudently, I responded, "What happens if you never have children? You mean there won't be anything in life for you, and everything will be worthless?" He did not reply.

When I was twelve I began studying commerce at the Kanuma Agricultural and Commercial School. Every morning I walked the nearly four kilometers to school with a friend, talking all the way. Time and again we discussed questions like the meaning of life and its greatest worth. Whether money or social position or fame or glory is most important is up to the individual. Even as a child, I always wondered whether those things were actually of the highest value. I could never find an answer to the question I had posed myself: If it was impossible to attain these external things for some reason, would this mean that a person's life then became meaningless, a blank? When I heard Ueki Rōshi say, "The ultimate Way is not difficult, it simply rejects discrimination," I was elated.

After I grew up I read an early Buddhist text called the *Dhammapada* (Words of the Doctrine). The twentieth chapter is called "The Path." The first verse reads: "Among the virtues, freedom from attachment is the best." I was deeply moved to discover, when Ueki Rōshi died in May 1967, that he had left nothing to mark his ninety-seven years, neither letters nor possessions. On the evening of his private funeral it happened, while I was having a cup of saké with Ganshō Suzuki, the present temple head, that I heard a complaint aired about Ueki Rōshi's Dharma successor and the then temple head, Kokan Hayashi Rōshi, that he never left any money at all in the temple when he went out, making it impossible to pay even incidental bills. "Why didn't you mention this directly to the Rōshi?" I asked. I saw him hesitate. "Isn't it related to 'the ultimate Way is not difficult; it simply rejects discrimination?' " The next morning as I was passing in front of Suzuki Rōshi's room he called me in and apologized. This is exactly what can be expected of a Zen priest; he is able to recognize his own mistakes at once.

UEKI RŌSHI'S EYES

Around the end of July 1938 I was again staying at Unganji Temple, immersed in the practice of Zen. One day we students were walking grouped around the Rōshi in the temple garden. Suddenly, he turned to me, walking beside him on his left, and asked, "Iizuka, why do you look at my face all the time?" The sudden question left me at a loss for words.

The Rōshi did not push the question further but continued walking as if nothing had happened.

At that time, though I was absorbed in my Zen meditation, I was constantly asking myself what made this remarkable Rōshi different from the rest of us, and I found my eyes fixed not so much on his face as on his eyes. Always mild of expression, his eyes alone were piercing. They made you think of a fine blade, and I felt he had no enemy in the world. There was not the slightest shadow of anxiety, indecision or bewilderment in him. He seemed to possess an absolute tranquillity of mind, such that no enemy in the universe, living or not, could cause him the slightest tremor.

Such were the Rōshi's eyes. They fascinated me beyond all reason, and I was continually trying to find out what lay in their depths, the nature of the reality they held. I suddenly realized that they might be concealing the secret of that "enlightenment" I was seeking.

Most of those studying Zen at Unganji were university students. Every summer there would be around thirty of them staying there. When the Rōshi threw his sudden question at me, he did not seem to mind that I did not answer, but continued walking as if nothing had happened. But something caught at my heart, and I wondered whether he realized that I was particularly interested in his eyes and that I was always searching for what lay in their depths. I have never in all my life met anyone with insight such as Ueki Rōshi possessed.

Sometime later, I believe it was the third time I visited the Rōshi privately to discuss my koan, I had no sooner entered his room and bowed before him, about four meters from where he was sitting, than he said in a low but distinct voice, "You will penetrate it, you know." I was speechless with admiration for his perspicacity. Did he actually know that I was about to reach the very core? It was only later that I recalled that one of the six superhuman powers of an enlightened being is the ability to perceive the hearts and minds of others. What struck me particularly was that, just a moment after such an exhibition of acuteness, the Rōshi would have let go of what he had said, and no trace would remain.

From the autumn of 1942 it was arranged that I would stay at Zuiganji Temple in Matsushima at the invitation of Jōten Miura Rōshi. Just before going there, I visited Ueki Rōshi at Unganji to pay my respects and asked him, rather impudently, how good a teacher Miura Rōshi was. The Rōshi replied, "He's like freshly made noodles, just that." I realized how apt the description was when I met Miura Rōshi a few months later. The world has many different kinds of Zen teachers.

Ueki Rōshi's eyes were as sharp as blades of bamboo grass and filled with conviction. Yet there was nothing deep within them. There was nothing, and thinking that there was something was an illusion. By nothing, I do not mean, in the ordinary way of thinking, that nothing existed; I mean, rather, that no dust smeared the mirror of his mind, that it was in the state of "nothingness" where all is wiped clean and beautifully polished. Such a burnished state comes only of the "nothingness" attained through training, day in and day out. Such training is something that is carried out intentionally and passionately, mediated by the concentrated chanting of the *Heart Sutra* dozens of times morning and evening. By this means the inner consciousness is perfectly cleansed, which I term "polished." It is the same process as Kūkai's repeated intonation of mantras.

THE HIGHEST WAY OF LIFE

Twelve hundred years separate us from Kūkai (774–835), the master of Japanese esoteric Buddhism, and it is therefore difficult to verify the truth of my statement above that training to perfect the personality through numerous repetitions of the *Heart Sutra* is the same as Kūkai's attainment through the repetition of mantras, mystical phrases believed to contain sacred power.

All the same, numerous sources remain concerning Kūkai's life and personality, which allow us to make some hypotheses at least. We have a large number of works that he himself wrote, such as *Sangō shiiki* (Indications of the Goals of the Three Teachings), an essay comparing Confucianism, Taoism, and Buddhism that he produced when he was twenty-four, and *Jūkūshinron* (The Ten Stages of the Development of Mind), a deeply philosophical work he wrote at sixty, as well as an anthology made after his death called *Shōryōshū* (Collected Works of Prose and Poetry of Kūkai). We also possess numerous examples of his calligraphy. Together, these permit us to appraise his life to a certain extent. Kūkai is one of the most famed calligraphers in Japanese history, and today many of his masterpieces are available to us in reproduction, allowing us to verify his greatness with our own eyes.

Kūkai is also known as a person who exhibited remarkable, even superhuman, abilities. He was not a great man from the first, but he became one as a result of his lifelong religious training. We can imagine the extent of his endeavors here when we read his anguished confession in the *Shōry-ōshū,* "I cried several times standing at the crossroads." Many centuries later, Myōchō (1282–1337), founder of the great Kyoto Zen temple of Daitokuji and now better known by his title of Kōzen Daitō Kokushi, was to write, "Believe the Way, I say, for Shaka does not naturally appear." Myōchō encourages people to believe in the teachings, for a great religious figure such as Śākyamuni does not appear naturally, or is not born great, as it were; but even ordinary people such as ourselves can, through training, attain greatness as human beings.

According to his biography, Kūkai came across a Buddhist sutra called the *Kōkūzō gumonji no hō* (its full title means "Ākāśagarbha Bodhisattva's power-filled, wish-fulfilling, supreme mind dhāranī technique for seeking hearing and retention") at the age of eighteen and trained according to its teachings. This sutra, No. 1145 in the Taishō Canon, contains about 2,150 characters and was translated from the original Sanskrit into Chinese by Śubhākarasimha (637–735), the first patriarch of esoteric Buddhism in China.

The sutra begins with a short sentence transliterated from the Sanskrit, the *dhāranī.* It goes on to recommend that the practitioner take up his meditation in a quiet, secluded place and repeat the dhāranī in sets of three, three, one, one, one, one, seven, twenty-five, three, three and one, with each group interspersed with meditation and ritual actions. In the course of this practice the dhāranī will be repeated one million times. No rest period may be taken during the practice, which indicates the extent to which the practitioner must be absorbed in it. Successful completion of the practice will result in the attainment of a perfect memory, which perhaps indicates that the practitioner has achieved supernatural powers. A person who has completed the practice can immediately understand, memorize, and retain virtually any written matter. Thus, his or her powers of memorization are unsurpassed. A professor of Chinese literature at Tokyo University who has studied *The Ten Stages of the Development of Mind* estimates that Kūkai has quoted from more than six hundred Chinese sources, which suggests he must have had powers of memory far beyond the normal ability. In an age when there were no copiers or pens or notebooks, Kūkai was clearly unique.

What I am concerned with here is not so much the *dhāranī* or any specific meditation or ritual action, but rather how a person can become thoroughly purified, right through to his life's essence. Kūkai's reciting of the *dhāranī* a million times is no different at all, I think, from Ueki Rōshi's absorbed recitation of the *Heart Sutra* dozens of times every morning and evening for sixty years, interspersed with intercessions for ancestors and others. I have never met any person as sensitive and as widely knowledgeable as Ueki Rōshi, or any one else as capable as he of forgetting the self and praying for the happiness of others. I see in Ueki Rōshi the highest way of human life.

THOROUGHLY PURIFYING THE SELF

As Wilhelm Windelband correctly states in his *Einleitung in die Philosophie* (Introduction to Philosophy), "Life is but a single existence." When you die, your life ends. The essential fact of human existence is that it occurs only once. You may say that everyone knows this, but do you yourself live each day in this knowledge? Many people in the world indeed pursue their lives as if they will live to be a thousand. I truly realized this truth, as I mentioned above, in the spring of 1939, when I was twenty-one, and that first exposure to Windelband's work sent a shock to the core of my being. Until then I had thought, much like Kobayashi Issa, that dying was something that happened to other people, not to me, and the impact of those words made me weep all through the night.

An important question then occurred to me. How should I spend this life that I was to live only once? Of course, I had been visiting Ueki Rōshi at Unganji and practicing Zen meditation there since the summer I was sixteen, but there remained within me much that was too easy-going, and until I entered university I maintained an unreal attitude toward things. It is said that Old Man Shōju (1642–1721) had his enlightenment confirmed by the Zen master Shidō Bunan (1603–1676) when only nineteen, but at the same age I was a mass of confusion. During the summer I was twenty-one, Ueki Rōshi allowed me to visit him formally for the first time to discuss my meditation. I had waited four years for that moment. It had been a long, long wait. At last I would receive a koan and have the opportunity to discuss the state of my practice.

But enough of this chatter about myself. I have a question for you. How do you want to live your life? Edmund Husserl (1859–1938), the teacher of probably the greatest philosopher of this century, the German Martin Heidegger (1889–1976, author of *Being and Time*), divided all human activity into two poles, the subjective and the objective. The former he called *noesis* ("the process of perceiving") and the latter *noema* ("the object of perception"). Human beings generally live with emphasis on the objective pole, that is, the objective world as perceived by our minds. An example is asking ourselves how to drive a car or how we should best answer a particular question. To perceive the realm of objects from our own point of view involves technique and theory. In short, all the sorts of things examinations ask us require a precise grasp of the world of objects, the objective pole. How can we refine our knowledge to the level at which we can gain full marks? It depends on the extent to which we should purify ("empty") the subjective of the objective. It seems that many people have not realized that fact.

For decades (in fact, just thirty-two years) I continued my observation of Ueki Rōshi. What was it that made him so sensitive? Why was he so discerning? Why was he so sharp? Why was he so rich in insight? The conclusion I reached was that he had become what he was because he was concerned every day with thoroughly purifying ("emptying") his subjective self. His life was nothing else than this. Nothing else at all. It was amazing.

As he approached death, Zen Master Takuan (1573–1645) penned the following as his final poem:

> As fast as the flintstone sparks
> Like a flash of lightning
> In the twinkling of an eye
> The subjective self is jettisoned and turned about.

The perspicacity of the poem explains why Iemitsu, the third Tokugawa shogun, admiring his approach to life, built him a large temple called Tōkaiji in the capital of Edo (present-day Tokyo).

It is strange, but I have heard that Ueki Rōshi's disciple Tetsuzen Watanabe did not, even at the last, have his enlightenment certified by his master. His certification was eventually granted by the master of Tōkaiji. The world of Zen is very harsh.

SEEKING ALWAYS TO GO FORWARD

The samurai Kuroda Josui (1546–1604) won many victories for his suzerain Toyotomi Hideyoshi and took part in the Korean campaigns of 1592 and 1597. Due to his enmity with Ishida Mitsunari, who supported the interests of Hideyoshi's heir, he sided with the hegemon Tokugawa Ieyasu at the Battle of Sekigahara in 1600 and helped secure Kyushu for him. His eldest son Nagamasa (1568–1623), lord of Fukuoka Castle in Kyushu, was known throughout the country for his military prowess. It is said that Kuroda Josui first wanted to master the Japanese poetic form known as *waka* but that he later decided to study to be a warrior and came to excel in strategy.

It was Kuroda Josui who devised the ethical code called the "five principles of water." I did not hear about it when I was young, but was taught it later by Ueki Rōshi. The code considers the nature of water from five angles and draws ethical comparisons from each of these principles.

The first principle states that water will continue flowing without stop until it finds its own level. Yes, this is certainly true. Water does not stop flowing, even for a second, as it seeks lower and lower ground. His greatness stems from the fact that he made use of this excellent principle in his own life. Perhaps you think it too obvious and easily forgotten. But are we all continually asking ourselves how we should best lead our lives and looking at ourselves critically, not resting for even a moment as we continually cultivate ourselves? If we are not, we fall far short of Kuroda Josui. Are we able to pull ourselves up when life is not sufficiently satisfactory? Our future hangs on this point.

Look at the people around you who are older than you. Do they suggest to you that, on the whole, they are cultivating themselves without a moment's rest? I do not mean breathlessly or angrily. I am referring to their mental attitude. Recently, at the funeral of Kiyoshi Kurosawa, someone commented to the effect that Kurosawa had lived always imposing a challenging subject. This spoke to me, for seeking always to go forward without a minute's rest is not something that results from a decision; rather, such a search has to come from far deeper within, from a place that exists before any decision, or it cannot be successful. It is this that separates a great person from an ordinary one.

In January 1990 I went to Okinawa, where I visited a Zen temple called Kōzenji. Its resident priest, Sōgen Sakiyama, showed me a scroll written by the late head of Engakuji Temple in Kamakura, Asahina Sōgen Rōshi (1891–1979). Asahina Rōshi was a fine poet and calligrapher as well as a great Zen priest. It was under this master that Masaharu Iizuka, the current president of TKC, studied Zen as a youth. The scroll read:

Within this boundless universe
Are countless numbers of people.
How many of them
Are real?

Does "real" perhaps refer to those people who never cease in their endeavor to go forward?

What is the goal of this search? When I attended the funeral of Ueki Rōshi in the autumn of 1967, I visited the Rōshi's quarters to greet Ueki's Dharma successor, Kokan Hayashi Rōshi. In the alcove behind Kokan Rōshi hung a scroll containing an elegy for Ueki Rōshi written by Asahina Rōshi:

> He surpasses even Kōhō in nobility.
> His Zen was simple, elegant, liberated.
> On the peak of the Eastern Mountain he was concerned about the life [of the people] and [the prospects for] the Way [of buddhahood].
> Scolding the rain, abusing the wind, for ninety years.

Asahina Rōshi describes Ueki Rōshi as a great Zen master, surpassing even Unganji Temple's founder Kōhō Kennichi (1241–1316), also known by his posthumous title, Bukkoku Kokushi, the third son of Emperor Go-Saga. Ueki's style of Zen was simple yet classical in its freedom. For over ninety years he lived at one with the universe on the Eastern Mountain of Unganji, always concerned for the future of the people and of Buddhism.

3

The Fundamentals of Mind

SEEKING THE TRUE SELF

What Is the True Self?

Many people believe that the image they have of themselves in their head or mind is their true self. This assumption should be considered a little more carefully. The "self" you paint in your mind is a self which has been painted, not the self which paints. People become discouraged because of the mistakes this painted image of the self makes and the ignorance it exhibits; they suffer, and hate themselves. What they are actually doing is playing a sort of game based on a misapprehension. I think there are a good number of people working at TKC who play this game of deception. They have never tried to discover the truth about themselves, or to examine themselves seriously concerning their real self.

In 1917, the Austrian physician and founder of psycho-analysis Sigmund Freud published his *Vorlesungen zur Ein-führung in die Psychoanalyse* (Introductory Lectures on Psy-choanalysis), in which he wrote, "The Self is by no means the master of its own house" ("Ich nachweisen will, das es nicht einmal Herr ist im eigenen Hausen," p. 226). What led him to this conclusion? He had read the works of the nineteenth-century German philosopher Arthur Schopen-hauer, in particular his *Parerga und Paralipomena,* and knew that human behavior is not connected with cognition. Ac-cording to Schopenhauer, that which we call human behav-ior is decided by means of an inner impulse ("innern Im-puls") originating in instinct and is not based on such things as cognition (p. 559). Schopenhauer came to this conclusion through an investigation of people's dreams. Freud was stim-ulated by Schopenhauer to absorb himself, too, in the study of dreams and neurosis. He discovered that a person's ac-tions are determined not by the self the self thinks exists, but by the unconscious mind deep within. He was convinced that the human consciousness had a three-layered structure consisting of consciousness, unconsciousness, and precon-sciousness. He published these results in *Introductory Lec-tures on Psychoanalysis.* The correctness of his theories has been established by modern cerebral medicine. Conscious-ness as defined by Freud is now called surface consciousness, and his unconsciousness and preconsciousness are termed subconsciousness and deep consciousness, respectively. Ac-cording to modern cerebral medicine, the surface conscious-ness is governed by something called the cerebral neocortex system, which includes functions such as thought and creativity. Human behavior, in turn, is known to be determined by the cerebral limbic system. (See Toshihiko Tokizane, *Ningen de aru koto* [Being Human]). What we have always thought of as "self" is not that which controls behavior, but only an idea of the self. Zen's greatest concern is the nature of this true self. Zen may be considered the search for the true self on the very field of life itself.

My overriding concern is the quest for Self. About five centuries before the present era, Socrates stood in the marbled streets of Athens and cried out, "Youth, know yourself!" This knowledge of Self is in itself the theme of Zen. It is a far greater issue than we imagine. We have only to think of the young man who threw himself to death over the Kegon Falls with the words, "Life is a mystery," to understand its scope. Ascertaining who we truly are is the starting point of all things in our life.

THE WORKINGS OF MIND

The mind works in wonderful ways. Nevertheless, perhaps because it has no form, few people are observing it. In particular, they cannot deal with the idea of the "true self," because it indicates the self as subject. This poses a problem, for human beings cannot perceive the subjective self objectively. In a world in which the self cannot be seen objectively, the fact of the subjective self poses a difficult-to-penetrate barrier. Given this, there is no method other than "knowing the self." This is exemplified by the Zen expression "knowing by oneself whether it is hot or cold." Knowledge must be achieved through personal experience. Even so, few people have ever managed to know their true self. It is not surprising, therefore, that even the Buddha took six years to penetrate the question.

A further source of difficulty is that, as this formless mind acts, it easily forms habits and customs. Someone whose gaze is constantly fixed thirty centimeters in front of him or herself will never see beyond the horizon. Such habits are truly troublesome, because they are not tangible and so remain unrecognized. Because we do not realize they are there, they adhere spontaneously all the more firmly. Buddhism calls these "residual mental habits." Emancipating ourselves from them is a decisive step on the path toward enlightenment. Since they are mental habits that are deeply impressed in the physical makeup, they cling obstinately to the ignorant mind and are not easily wiped away. A person who is conscious of a conflict with these residual habits in the life of the mind can be said to have arrived at the threshold of enlightenment.

Emancipation from habits of this type can be achieved only by observing the mind. Once we are able to observe the mind, all we have to do is work to acquire an ability to dwell constantly at peace within our original mind. This is a state beyond physical characteristics or form, capable of penetrating in every direction. To dwell knowingly in this state is to work repeatedly to bring the mind to its constant turning point. It is to enter a realm of incredible tranquillity, a state where no stress exists, representing the very advent of a world at peace.

Late in his life, Goethe confessed in conversation with Johann Peter Eckermann that he had always returned to the mind's turning point. He saw the state of no-mind as a continual returning to this point. We are reminded that not only Goethe but all the great people of history returned repeatedly to the state of no-mind. My master Ueki Rōshi, too, was certainly such a person. As a result of the profundity and strictness of his training, he was able to return to a state of no-mind in an instant, but because he did not cling to it, he could penetrate anything without obstruction. He lived in a state of absolute freedom. That he lived to the age of ninety-seven was perhaps due to the fact that he never accumulated stress. However busy he seemed to be outwardly, he was at rest within and so was never reduced to being bone tired. Shinran wrote in the Shōshinge that to know life and death truly was to be in a state of nirvana. Ueki Rōshi lived in this way; he departed for the afterworld disinterestedly, knowing that dying is a return. Close to thirty years have passed since then, but even now I cherish his memory keenly.

I began by speaking about the workings of the mind. My point is that I think it regrettable that most people rarely observe the workings of their mind. It saddens me to think of promising young people who cling to the phenomena that surround them. They are weighed down by residual mental habits that lodge themselves immovably in the mind. We live only once. We should therefore live that life to the full in the freedom that comes of enlightenment.

ILLUSION

The philosopher Arthur Schopenhauer wrote, "Human beings are animals who are fond of illusion." Certainly illusion is an overwhelming characteristic of humanity. Perhaps only one in a hundred thousand or a million are free from it. Whatever the actual number, it is very small.

Other animals suffer from illusions, but it is particularly true of human beings, perhaps because, as Pascal put it, "Man is a thinking reed." The ability to think is a peculiarly human quality. Someone who is placed in a difficult situation, for example, will worry much more than another person who takes a more objective standpoint, and act in a way that is difficult for others to understand. In recent years the newspapers have reported cases of young boys and girls jumping to their deaths off tall buildings. To choose to die as soon as some minor trouble occurs has its origins in a mighty illusion, though some might say they were benefiting society by helping to decrease Japan's high population. I think it is from around the age of twenty-two or twenty-three, however, that people realize what a rare and valuable thing it is to be born into this world as a human being, since human life makes up but a small proportion of living things, and being born human is itself such a result of chance (though Hegel speaks of the inevitability of chance).

When I read Windelband's *Introduction to Philosophy*, I spent all of one night in tears, having come upon his question on the nature of life and his answer, "Life is but a single existence." It is probably in our early twenties that we have the most opportunities to think seriously about our own life existence. The *Analects* record that, when Confucius was asked by a disciple, "Master, what is death?" he answered, "You don't know anything about life yet, so how can you know death?" I myself believe this to be a story made up by his disciples, for it is a question that permits no simple, clear-cut answer.

In his famous autobiography the English economist John Stuart Mill (1806–1873) wrote that whether or not a person becomes successful in life depends on whether he has, at around the age of twenty-three, thought about the basic questions of human life. There is, I believe, no question of the validity of his argument. It is of utmost difficulty that we investigate thoroughly who we are and encounter what the Buddha called the "True Self." The majority of people tend to lose interest and give up halfway, putting the question aside before they have reached any conclusion. The earliest sutras, contained in the Pali *Nikāyas* and the Chinese *Āgamas,* tell us that the Buddha was in his late twenties when he began to feel the world's transience acutely. That he was not so troubled until later than usual was perhaps due to his protected upbringing (his father was a local ruler). Schopenhauer, in the fourth volume of his *Collected Works,* comments that those who perfect their self-protective techniques too early rarely become successful in life. It is rather the people who still have not done so by around their forties, who are always imposed upon and taken in by others, who eventually become successful. There is in the East the expression, "Great talents mature late," which we can take to mean that truly great people first achieve success only in their later years. In this sense Schopenhauer's words would seem to be correct.

However we look at it, discovering one's true self is crucial. Only by doing so can we escape the net of illusions and begin seeing things constantly as they really are. Illusions grow from even the minute extraneous thoughts that settle in the mind. Even thoughts as small as the tiny particles of dust that float in the atmosphere prevent us from seeing the truth of things. Whether or not we attain the state of what physics calls an "absolute vacuum" in our heads or minds determines the fruit of spiritual training. It is said that a carpenter called Heishir Anbara attained that state in three days and nights, an amazing feat.

SEEKING THE SELF

Most people experience a wide variety of mental states, from defeat, humiliation, bitterness, despair, anger, and jealousy to pleasure and feelings of success and happiness. The Buddha described people's minds as being of 1,240 different types. I have never made a count, but I do know I have experienced a great number of moods and feelings. When I was in elementary school and never allowed to take part in athletic festivals, in particular, I envied the others from the bottom of my heart and frequently felt jealousy and defeatism. At times I was in such low spirits that I even contemplated suicide.

I truly believe that a person's fortune is decided by his or her mental attitude. Perhaps because of this, people have continued since ancient times to seek to know the nature and essence of the mind. Socrates' "Know yourself" means, "Know the essence of your own mind." Seeking the self is the greatest study in life, and it can even be said that, unless this question is solved, a person's life cannot be considered satisfactory. At the same time, there is nothing in the world more difficult than seeking the self.

What makes seeking the self difficult is that the mind has no shape or form. Professor Shinohara of Tōhoku University used to say, "The mind's only attribute is *intendieren* [intention]." Since the mind is not quantifiable or measurable, it is difficult to understand. Zen Master Lin-chi I-hsüan (d. 867)

said, "The mind is shapeless and penetrates the ten directions." If we contemplate this statement, we will gradually
come to understand what Self is. More than seven hundred
years ago there lived a Zen priest called Bassui (1327–1387).
In his recorded writings, he describes the essence of Zen as
"penetrating one's mind," which is to say, gaining penetrating knowledge of one's own mind. Penetrating one's mind is,
I think, what is meant by the search for self. It is to probe
the roots of the mind.

To explain what I mean by probing the mind's roots I
must first mention Kant's *Kritik der reinen Vernunft* (Critique of Pure Reason), published in 1781. Here Kant completely refuted the representative view of human cognition
expounded by David Hume (1711–1776) in his *Treatise of
Human Nature* (1739), pointing out the errors in his argu-
ments. Hume had said, "The ideas I form are exact representations of the impressions I felt" (Everyman's Library edition, vol. 1, p. 12). All human ideas, Hume says, are
representations made, via sensation, of things existing in the
world about us. Kant, however, rebutted this view. Briefly
stated, he said that human beings do not know what exists
outside themselves, but only make constructions of the outside world through sensation. What is without is things in
themselves ("Ding an sich"); this stimulates the objects of
sensation, which constitute images of outward reality, not
exact representations. He wrote, "I do not know, nor is there
any need for me to know, what things in themselves might
be" ("Was die Dinge an sich sein mögen, weiss ich nicht und
brauche es auch nicht zu wissen" [Dr. H. A. Gerstenberg
Verlag, 1973, p. 234]). No one since has been able to over-
turn Kant's theory of cognition. It follows that seeking the

self is the search for the subjective self (master of oneself) that constitutes cognition of the outside world by means of sensation, in other words, the mind's essence. What Kant discovered had in fact already been realized well over 2,000 years before by the Buddha, meditating in the forests of northern India.

HOW TO SEEK THE SELF

Seeking the self means searching for the mind's essence. I would like to speak here a little more about how we can go about that task.

History offers us numerous examples of people who spent decades in their search for self, and many of them never reached enlightenment at all. Ānanda, the Buddha's disciple and personal attendant for more than forty-five years, had not yet attained enlightenment when the Buddha died, and he is described as standing in the doorway weeping and crying as the Buddha passed away (Nakamura Hajime, *Gotama Buddha*). A mistake in undertaking the search for self results in a huge loss in human life. Though I myself am poor in human experience, it is out of this concern that I venture to speak of seeking the self.

From another perspective, the search for self is a search for the essence of the self as an existence within the cosmos. In this sense it includes the requirement that we understand ourselves in the context of both the world and the universe, while we seek the essence of the self in the narrow sense of the term. The compelling question then becomes how we should best set about doing this, bearing in mind the need not to take an inordinate amount of time about it. Masters of old have left many instructions for us with respect to this. There is no need to examine them all; it is more logical and a more economical use of time, I feel, to grasp those that treat the substance of the matter. One work that focuses on how to seek the self is *Ch'an-kuan ts'e-chin* (Incentives for Breaking Zen Barriers), compiled in 1600 by a Chinese priest named Chu-hung (1535–1615). The young Hakuin, it is said, treasured this work and read it constantly.

The Sōtō stream of Zen Buddhism is generally considered to encourage "just sitting" *(shikan taza)* as its core method, but a reading of the *Shōbō genzō* (Treasury of the Eye of the True Dharma) by Sōtō's founder, Zen master Dōgen (1200–1253), suggests strongly that conundrums, or "cases," known as *koan* were also used extensively. There are hundreds of koan; seventeen hundred is the most frequently quoted number. In fact they are possibly countless. One of the most famous of them is the "Mu" koan of the Chinese master Chao-chou (778–897). A later master, Ta-hui Tsung-kao (1089–1163), even stated that this was the only koan that was really necessary. When I started formal Zen training, this was the koan I received from my master, Ueki Rōshi; I never received any other. In effect, since the koan is only a device to help the student seek the essential self, there is no meaning in assigning large numbers of them. Since some Zen masters of lesser ability cannot perceive the mental state of their students clearly, however, they issue them many different koan in order to observe their reactions from various angles. Verifying their own judgment by these means, they are able to guide their students. It is not easy to judge the quality of a master, since the ability to do so depends on the observer's own capabilities. Masters like Akizuki Ryōmin place considerable value on the koan, although Ryōmin's vision is out of focus, I feel. To return to my original point, though, koan like Chao-chou's "Mu" or the koan that asks what our face was before our parents were born are very apt.

Chao-chou's "Mu" goes as follows. One day a priest monk asked Chao-chou, "Has a dog the buddha nature [the ability to attain buddhahood]?" Chao-chou answered, "Mu" ("no," or "nothingness"). The point of the koan is this "mu." At some other time Chao-chou answered the same question with "yes," by which we know that his "mu" does not simply mean "no" in contrast to "yes," but rather contains no sense of relativity at all. It is the "mu" that transcends all relativity, the Great Nothingness that goes beyond the simple positive and negative. We should place this conundrum firmly in the forefront of our mind and investigate it single-mindedly, without any distraction of thought. This means we can never rest. Night and day we must pursue our search, throwing ourselves utterly into the task with a willingness to risk our life itself to accomplish it. Every action, every appearance in our daily life becomes the grounds for our quest. The most important factor in determining whether the way to enlightenment is long or short is the fervor of our endeavors.

NO-THOUGHT

I spoke in the preceding section of three points of great importance in the search for self: spiritual themes, such as Chao-chou's "Mu" koan; the need for a committed and serious outlook regarding the search; and a commitment to conducting this search in the very midst of daily life activity.

I would like to speak a little further on the topic, to make it as relevant and easily understood as possible.

The reason koan like Chao-chou's "Mu" are so useful is because they are direct and do not require wasteful thought. Since the essence of Zen is the search for the essential self and verification of the Truth underlying it, koan that cut deeply and directly into one's true mind are far more effective than koan that merely confuse thought. Ta-hui Tsung-kao's contention that only Chao-chou's koan is really necessary is therefore entirely reasonable. His "mu" is not "nothing" as opposed to "something" or "nothing" as a relative concept or idea. It transcends relativity, demands that we take hold of absolute, essential "nothingness." The koan has nothing to do with seeking any definition or interpretation of "mu." It refers rather to "mu" that transcends all relative difference, requiring us to seek "mu" as substance, rather than the limited "mu" of the word. Since the concept of "mu" acts as the medium for seeking out the essential "mu," we start off with the sound of "What is mu" constantly in our mind, ringing like an alarm bell, until our whole body becomes "mu." Only then can we go beyond "mu" as a concept. Put another way, we come to experience the essential state of "mu," where the self no longer holds any objects at all in the mind. Such an understanding is extremely important in the first place, for it allows us to use the time we need for our endeavor more economically. Since ours is an age of educational advances, we must be able to understand ahead of time how the mind is constructed and what mental state we should be aiming at with respect to it. When I studied Zen under Miura Rōshi of Zuiganji Temple in 1942 and 1943, I severely criticized his style of Zen training as being old-fashioned. Why couldn't we be taught directly, I asked, about the mind's construction and advised about the proper state of mind we should be aiming toward. The Rōshi was unable to reply; men like him only know how to teach within the inertia of tradition.

The state of holding no objects at all in the mind is termed "no-thought" in Zen Buddhism. The Buddha called it the state of mind of a Tathāgata (a buddha), the state of one who has attained enlightenment. Such a mind penetrates all things. I wrote above that we can seek such a mind in the very midst of the daily activity of life. Yet, since such a mind contains not the slightest trace of self-consciousness or self-centeredness, since it is in a state of complete non-consciousness and non-attachment, to apply the word "seek" to it seems somewhat superfluous. Since the mind of non-attachment, "no-mind," exists within all daily actions and phenomena, there is no need for a special mind construct such as "seeking." Calculating, auditing, cleaning, even pouring tea, all aspects of life are in fact activities carried out within "no-mind." In other words, "no mind" means to live completely at one with all the objects of life. This represents the most concentrated state of mind, in which no objects at all intrude on the mind (the mind is attached to nothing). The Pali *Nikāyas* describe the state of mind of the Tathāgata as an "objectless concentration of mind" (*Some Sayings of the Buddha*, trans. F. L. Woodward, Oxford University Press, 1955, p. 340). This was the state of mind attained by the Buddha as a result of his desperate six-year search.

Zen Master Hakuin, who revived Japanese Rinzai Zen in the nineteenth century, studied under a layman called Old Man Shōju, who lived at Iiyama in the present-day Nagano

Prefecture and who had himself studied under another layman, a former innkeeper at Sekigahara who received the
title Zen Master Shidō Bunan (1603–1676) after his death.
Neither man was an ordained priest. Shidō Bunan described
the enlightened state of mind in a poem:

> A dewdrop as it is,
> When on an [autumn] maple leaf,
> Is a scarlet jewel.

The mind of one who has succeeded in the search for self
remains constantly like a clear and empty sky, like a pane of
transparent glass. How about it, readers? Shall we try to
attain this state together, bearing in mind that we live only
once?

JOIN NOT TWO THOUGHTS TOGETHER

Since so many people fail in their quest for the self, let me
speak a little longer about how we should go about the
search. It is easy to talk about things such as "no-thought,"
living constantly at one with all objects of life without letting
one's consciousness become attached to any of those objects.
Unfortunately, it is much more difficult to achieve. We need
to train ourselves implacably, but because we are creatures
of words and concepts, we find ourselves overwhelmed with
ideas one after the other, and the state of "no-thought"
retreats further and further into the distance.

Zen Master Hakuin taught that the quickest way to attain
a state of "no-mind" was not to join two thoughts together.
When a man sees an attractive woman, for example, he
thinks, "Wow, she's pretty!" That is his initial thought—

and his most vulnerable moment. In most cases, the man then goes through a succession of thoughts about how he would like to meet her, embrace her, or whatever. In other words, the initial thought develops into a chain of thoughts, all strung together. This is no good as far as Zen training is concerned. The second thought to arise should not be linked to the initial thought. The Zen student has to work on breaking the train after the initial thought arises. If this is accomplished, strangely enough, the initial thought dies down and eventually disappears. As such results are achieved more and more frequently, the mind spontaneously enters a state of "no-mind." Ueki Rōshi would always say such training needed a hundred polishings, a thousand forgings. If we stop after having achieved no particular result four or five times, we will never in all our life become an adept. Thus, it requires a hundred polishings, a thousand forgings. Masters of old also used the expression "a thousand polishings, ten thousand forgings." Their point was not that there is any particular meaning in counting the number, but that a student should practice as frequently as possible. They did not hand down such expressions with the intention of fooling us. When we realize that their words stem from their own hard-attained experience, we are inspired by their loving concern to make every effort in our own training.

This teaching of Hakuin's about not joining two thoughts together, which I learned as a youth from Ueki Rōshi, seems to have come, as I discovered later, from an expression in Chu-hung's *Incentives for Breaking Zen Barriers*, "Do not cause two thoughts to join further." Whatever the origin of the phrase, though, the practice of not joining two thoughts together is an essential point in training in everyday life, quite apart from koan study.

The sixth Zen patriarch in the lineage from Bodhidharma was called Hui-neng (638–713). He attained great enlightenment when his master, the Fifth Patriarch Hung-jen (601–674), lecturing in the middle of the night in a darkened room on the *Diamond Sutra*, came to the words, "Raise [that] thought without letting it settle on any particular thing." "Not letting the mind settle" means not allowing the mind to attach itself to any object, which is the same as not letting two thoughts join together. This is one of the most critically important points in Zen training. In youth people are overwhelmed by trouble and distress, and the mind is always scattered. When they are disappointed in love, for instance, they want to commit suicide. Before making such a decision, let us consider that our own life is the result of a continual process that began billions of years ago when living organisms first moved out of primeval seas onto land, mating and producing young, and the product of untold billions of ancestors. Faced with this mighty march of life, I feel we cannot take our life lightly and pass our days heedlessly, but that we should realize the origin of the spirit behind life in order to live our one and only life in a truly worthwhile manner.

PREVAILING OVER THE SELF

When we examine the expression "prevailing over the self" and are compelled to ask who it is that so prevails, we can only answer, using the common sense of the ordinary world, that it is the Self which prevails over the self. This is, I believe of great significance.

First, to say that the Self prevails over the self intimates that there are at least two selves. This refers to a physical self and one or more spiritual selves. This is a fundamental point.

I recall here Sigmund Freud's *Introductory Lectures on Psychoanalysis,* a compilation of twenty-eight of his lectures. The eighteenth ends with the words I quoted at the beginning of this chapter, "The Self is by no means the master of its own house." His assertion here is that consciousness of the self (now called "surface consciousness"), in which people have a sense of their own identity, is in fact not Self, the master of the personality. Freud was the first Western scholar to claim a three-layered structure of consciousness, but this idea originated in India, in Buddhism. A conscientious person, Freud admitted his debt in this to Schopenhauer's *Aphorismen zur Lebensweisheit* (Aphorisms Concerning Life's Wisdom, 1851), a book published many years after his life's work, *Die Welt als Wille und Vorstellung* (The World as Will and Representation, 1818). Human intellectual and behavioral choices, he says, are completely unrelated, and he concludes that human behavior is determined by means of an inner impulse (*Collected Works,* vol. 4, p. 559). As Sarvepalli Radhakrishnan (1888–1975) points out in a footnote on page 633 of the first volume of his *Indian Philosophy* (1923), however, this was not Schopenhauer's original idea but one derived from his reading of the *Upanishads* and the *Vedanta,* which had been a consolation to him since his youth. Buddhism has been called one of the Upanishadic schools, and it was the idea of the construction of the human consciousness found in Buddhist philosophy that was transmitted to Freud through Schopenhauer.

The view of the self as divided into two is found not only among Indian and European scholars but in the writings of the Chinese philosopher Wang Yang-ming as well. In Japan, Wang is famous for an aphorism contained in his *Ch'uan-hsi lu* (Instructions for Practical Living), which reads, "It is easy to overcome the bandits in the mountains, but it is not easy to overcome the bandits in the mind." He considered the human mind to be of a twofold construction involving what he called the original self and the self of the physical husk.

In modern times the mind is thought to consist of the surface consciousness and the deep consciousness. The latter determines human actions and behavior; it contains the "inner impulse" and releases limitless desires, which are expressed as various forms of behavior and action. Buddhism seeks to purify the deep consciousness, to penetrate emptiness. The Chinese Zen priest Wu-hsüeh Tsu-yüan (1226–1286), threatened with death by Mongol soldiers who broke into his temple, dictated the following as his death poem:

> Joyful to receive:
> Man is emptiness;
> The Dharma is emptiness.

To have realized emptiness in this way and to have incorporated it into his daily life as the basis for all his actions shows the degree of enlightenment he had attained. One who always lives having completely penetrated Wang Yang-ming's "original self" no longer has two dimensions to the self. The self is undivided and in a state of "emptiness." This is the greatest and most important destination in human life.

Zen Master Hakuin wrote, "Prevailing over the self in the space of one breath." Though this refers to a self that should be prevailed over, it does not indicate a state of enlightenment. When a person has purified the self to the utmost, cleansing the deep consciousness, there is no longer any need for a mind that prevails over the self. I consider that this is the basic premise of great human progress.

CAN THE HUMAN CHARACTER BE CHANGED?

Whether or not the human character can be changed is a question that has attracted great interest since ancient times.

When I was nineteen years old, my English teacher at Fukushima Higher Commercial School, the Englishman E. V. Gatenby, asked the class this question. I answered, audaciously, with what I had learned from Ueki Rōshi at Unganji Temple, that when a person becomes enlightened, he can change his own character. I was praised for my reply. In fact, I did not myself understand what I had said, for I was merely mouthing what I had heard Ueki Rōshi say and pretending that I knew. A fine scholar, Mr. Gatenby had authored a voluminous English dictionary for Japanese students as well as publishing a number of books in London. He had read virtually all of the works of Zen Master Hakuin. I remember him asking me at one time if I had read Hakuin's *O3rategama* (Embossed Teakettle) and being embarrassed at having to say I had not. Mr. Gatenby taught English literature at Tōhoku Imperial University as well.

Nevertheless, many people appear to think, and even to

believe, that it is impossible for the individual to change his character. I am sure you have come across men and women who say, without any uncertainty, that they are a particular type of person. Possibly you yourself say the same thing. Schopenhauer said this as well. In *Aphorisms Concerning Life's Wisdom,* he concluded, "For the character is completely unalterable" ("Denn der Charakter ist schlechthin inkorrigibel"; *Collected Works,* vol. 4, p. 542). This saying was a product of his later years by comparison with his famous work *The World as Will and Representation.* He seems to have drawn this conclusion from observing the way large numbers of people lived. All the same, he was mistaken.

The source of his error is clear when we investigate his reasons for reaching this conclusion. He wrote: "All human behavior flows from an inner principle [aus einem innern Prinzip fliessen], and according to this principle, a person will always do the same thing in the same circumstances, and cannot do any other." The problem lies in the nature of this inner principle. Buddhism speaks of *paribhavana* (lit. "patterns"), which stain the mind as residual mental habits. From birth onward, everyone accumulates countless experiences, within which habits of thought form unnoticed. When they take root, these are *paribhāvana.* Eliminating them is no easy thing and requires strenuous training.

We have seen how Schopenhauer read Upanishadic philosophy in Latin translation as a youth; Radhakrishnan notes Schopenhauer's love for the work in his *Indian Philosophy* and quotes Max Müller concerning it (vol. 2, p. 633). He should therefore have known about *paribhāvana.* Still, since the *Upanishads* are of great length and there are more than 320 partial translations of them in existence, he may well have misread something or overlooked it. All the same, a mistake is a mistake. People are released from the bonds of *paribhāvana* when they have had conclusive experience that the essence of the self is emptiness and have acquired the ability to shape their fate. Thus, people can change their character.

THE CONCLUSIVE EXPERIENCE OF EMPTINESS

How is it that people are released from the bonds of *paribhavana* when they have had conclusive experience that the essence of the self is emptiness and can acquire the ability to shape their destiny? Before I answer this question, I should first define what I mean by "conclusive experience that the essence of the self is emptiness." If we do not understand this clearly it is extremely difficult to go any further, for we will not understand the necessary reasoning underlying the connection between the experience of emptiness and the ability to shape fate.

Let us think about it quietly. First, from where were you born? Did you spring out of a cleft peach floating down a river, like Momotarō. Did you appear in the crook of a tree branch? Of course, you were born from your mother's body. As a result of the connection between your father and mother, your father's sperm fertilized your mother's egg, and you grew bigger and bigger over the months inside your mother's womb, until the time came for you to emerge and become a separate human being. This is an indisputable scientific fact. But let us consider the question a little further.

Where do human beings themselves come from? Even now, nobody knows the answer. No proof is anywhere to be found. Science tells us that a primate called *Ramapithecus* was a direct ancestor of the human race; this species had branched off from *Dryopithecus* during the Miocene epoch and differentiated and spread throughout India, southern China, East Africa, and Europe in the Pliocene epoch. Nevertheless, "though human beings have separated into a considerable number of races, the fact that all races can interbreed means that the human race is essentially one" (*Seibutsugaku jiten* [Dictionary of Biology], 3rd edition, Iwanami Shoten Publishers, p. 1226). The Indian *Vedas,* hymns and poems which go back some 3,500 years, also say that the human race has existed for billions of years.

The Christian Bible, on the other hand, says in Genesis 1:1 that "In the beginning, God created Heaven and Earth," then, on the sixth day of creation, "created Man in his own image" (1:27). The Book of John in the New Testament states, "In the beginning was the Word, and the Word was with God, and the Word was God" (1:1) and, "There was a man sent from God, whose name was John" (1:6). Truly, human beings are oblivious of their real origin.

What is clear is that one person must be born of two others, each of whom was likewise born of two others. After the same process has occurred over thirty generations, each person would theoretically have 536,870,912 ancestors. And if one generation is considered to be twenty-five years, our ancestors of thirty generations ago would have lived approximately 750 years ago. If we hypothesize that human beings emerged about one billion years ago, we must all be carrying the blood of countless billions of ancestors.

Zen, on the other hand, demands directly, "What was our own face before our mother and father were born?" Or it asks, "What is one phrase of the Pre-Voice (absolute reality)?" as in the seventh case recorded in the *Blue Cliff Record* (Chinese *Pi-yen lu;* Japanese *Hekiganroku*). Where were you before you parents were born? What did you look like before your parents were born? A deep investigation of these questions reveals that the essential Self has no form, no characteristics, that the true Self is "empty." This is the crux of the problem, that our true form is without odor, color, taste, or touch. It transcends time and space, dwelling in a place beyond all phenomenal appearance. Gradually, we learn to accept this and grow to understand, to the very depths of our being, that "emptiness" is our true state, our ultimate reality. This is no mere concept, but something that is understood physically as well. This is what I mean by a "conclusive experience of emptiness." It is not so difficult after all, is it?

TWO EPISTEMOLOGICAL VIEWS CONCERNING REALITY

Let us discuss now what it means to understand "emptiness" as our true state, not just as a concept but with all our being, which is to say, to have a conclusive experience of emptiness. It is incorrect to think that viewing the totality of phenomena is to exercise the functions of the eye alone, separate from the rest of the body. Similarly, if we wish to hear sound in its totality, we cannot separate the ear from the body and rely upon it alone. Sight, hearing, smell, taste, touch—all of the five senses—are no more than windows that allow human beings to make contact with the outside world.

There are two broad theories concerning the nature of knowledge and ideas. In *A Treatise of Human Nature* (1739), written when he was twenty-six, David Hume states,

"The ideas I form are exact representations of the impressions I felt" (Everyman's Library edition, vol. 1, p. 12). In other words, we "feel" the reality of the outer world through our senses, and what we "feel" are our ideas. He goes on to say, "This, then, is the first principle I establish in the science of human nature" (p. 16). This is the famous bundle theory of epistemology, a branch of philosophy. This view was overturned by Immanuel Kant, a lecturer at the University of Königsberg, in his *Kritik der reinen Vernunft* (Critique of Pure Reason), where he wrote, "After all, human beings do not know what exists outside themselves. Things in themselves [Ding an sich], which transcend the objects of sensual perception, contact and stimulate human sensations, where human beings construct the outside world." This is Kant's equally famous theory of epistemology.

Because dogs have a sense of smell thousands of times more sensitive than that of human beings, they are able to sniff out drugs hidden in luggage, and because birds have a sense of hearing thousands of times more acute than human beings, they can react to sounds that are inaudible to people and fly off simultaneously. I remember reading in Professor Shinohara's psychology text more than fifty years ago that human beings can hear sounds with a frequency of between thirty and thirty thousand oscillations a second; this is called their auditory range. This means that the human senses are extremely limited and unable to catch all that exists in the outer world. Nobody has ever been able to refute Kant's theory, but that is no reason to believe it to be absolutely correct. Directly after producing his *Critique of Pure Reason*, Kant wrote *Prolegomena*, in the preface of which he commented, "People will judge the *Critique of Pure Reason* improperly . . . [saying] that it is dry, difficult to understand, against all accepted ideas and, above all, verbose." He contended that "The *Critique of Pure Reason* is a completely new kind of scholarship and no one before has ever conceived of such" (". . . es eine ganz neue Wissenschaft sei, von welcher niemand auch nur den Gedanken vorher gefasst hatte" (*Immanuel Kant's Werke,* vol. 4, Verlag Dr. A. H. Gerstenberg Hildesheim, 1913, p. 10). However, the core of *Critique of Pure Reason,* the theory of knowledge, had already been expressed more than two thousand years previously by the Buddha. Kant had no reason to be conceited about what he had discovered, though of course he was probably completely ignorant of the fact.

Kant's theories were ignored by the German Karl Marx, who preferred Hume's empiricism. Marx employed the bundle theory in his *Misère de la philosophie* (The Poverty of Philosophy, 1847), written when he was twenty-nine, and made it the basis for a systematic theory. Marx, the natural-born revolutionary, used Hume's theory strategically as the theoretical basis to stimulate revolution.

But I have been derailed. Let us return to our discussion of "emptiness."

TO REALIZE EMPTINESS IS TO HAVE THE ABILITY TO CHANGE FATE

To have the conclusive experience of emptiness is to shift one's point of view from the limited, physical self to the great universe (emptiness). This might also be expressed as seeing emptiness within the depths of one's own mind. To realize emptiness is to smash the selfish and self-centered consciousness and to have the ground of the mind vanish like mist before the sun into the vastness of the universe. When the mind's ground vanishes in this way, we realize that the mind has neither inside nor outside.

Today, Buddhism has virtually disappeared from India, surviving only in Sri Lanka. In India, Hinduism is virtually supreme. One of the holiest books of Hinduism is the *Bhagavad Gita*. I possess a copy, in the original and in English translation, given me by a young Indian along with several other books. Unlike the *Upanishads*, the *Bhagavad Gita* does not form part of the *Vedas*. Interestingly, the *Bhagavad Gita* describes the state of mind of one who has, in one expression, "realized emptiness," or, in another, "attained enlightenment." Of particular importance is the sentence, "Distinctions such as inside and outside do not exist for him" (*Bhagavad Gita*, Tapovanam Publishing House, 1965, p. 342). In Hinduism, as in Buddhism, no distinction is made between the inside and the outside of mind. The text goes on to say, "One undivided, interminable consciousness is for him" (p. 342).

To have the conclusive experience of emptiness is to arrive at a state in which there is no distinction between the inside and outside of the mind, no sense of discrimination at all; consciousness of eternity exists therein. It is significant that the ground of thought is not within the mind, but vanishes into the great universe. *Paribhāvana,* which stain the mind as residual mental habits, become completely irrelevant. When thought rises freely and without restriction, fate can be formed equally freely. There is not the slightest obstruction remaining within the mind. "This state of Pure Consciousness is the goal of life," says the *Bhagavad Gita* (p. 181).

Please do not misunderstand. To realize emptiness conclusively and attain a firm understanding of one's own principle of action is to be able to live life in enlightened freedom. To become attached to the conclusive experience of emptiness, however, is a form of spiritual sickness. Having such an experience, and thereby becoming liberated in thought and action, enables one to mold his or her fate.

Schopenhauer asserted that because human beings are bound by an inner principle (*paribhāvana,* perhaps), they are unable to change their character. It is therefore strange that he wrote in the same work, "However, fate can improve itself" ("Das Schicksal aber kann sich bessern"; *Collected Works,* vol. 4, p. 380). He throws this comment in suddenly, but nowhere explains the reasoning behind it. To my mind, it is a contradiction and a mistake.

In the book *Loving Men for All the Right Reasons: Women's Patterns of Intimacy* (Dell Publishing, 1982) Yehuda Nir and Bonnie Maslin discuss the question of how women can attain true happiness by discovering their "patterns" *(paribhavana)* and reforming them. Character is variable, the authors say, and fate is therefore clearly variable too. What I particularly admire are their statements that people act according to unconscious desires, that their actions are determined by a fundamental principle, that the discovery of the true self brings about the possibility of change, and that asking the right questions about one's past and upbringing can reveal the source of conscious habits that adhere to the self and the roots of one's unconscious desires. There is a detailed discussion about how fate can be changed that extends for 273 pages.

TRANSCENDENTAL CONSCIOUSNESS

We normally live within knowledge based upon sensation. This means seeing people or things, hearing sounds, smelling odors, tasting food, and understanding the sizes of objects through our senses. This is called knowledge based on experience. In addition to this experiential understanding, however, we also possess transcendental understanding that is not directly related to the senses. This includes recognition of philosophical theories, for example. At the same time, human beings possess a *transcendental consciousness* (Transzendentales Bewusstsein). This is a consciousness that, though existing in the actual world of sensory knowledge, is neither bound nor regulated by the objects of sensation. In this sense, it has no connection with those objects. There are many people who have rich experiences of transcendental consciousness in their daily lives, yet who do not consciously take hold of them or consider them on a personal basis. Transcendental consciousness is also called "pure consciousness." It is of great importance that philosophers of the past have regarded the conscious comprehension of transcendental, or pure, consciousness and a devotion to living within it as human perfection. We can say that the goal of life is to actualize the self, or to perfect our personality. To ask what this "self" or "personality" is, however, leads us into difficult, controversial territory, for it does not denote our physical body, but refers rather to the idea of spirit.

It is highly desirable that we should be able to comprehend this transcendental, pure consciousness correctly in an aware manner in our own lives. This is quite simple to do once we have realized it, but in the unenlightened state transcendental consciousness cannot be comprehended easily within the twenty-four hours of every day. Zen Master Hakuin wrote in his *Zazen wasan* (Poems of Zen Meditation) that "it is like crying out for thirst in the midst of water." This teaches us that the transcendental consciousness is extremely close to us, but we tend not to consider this point in relation to our daily experience.

Forgive a personal note here, but one day when I was about twenty-two and staying at Unganji Temple, I was alone and gazing at the forest in the mountain fastnesses. My eyes were watching it, but I realized that no consciousness of it had appeared on the screen of my mind. Though I saw the mountain, I was not conscious of the mountain. I saw, but did not see, the mountain. That's it! I realized. I had discovered the existence of my transcendental, pure consciousness. I also understood as a result that I had always lived within that consciousness. Once understood, it turned out to be just daily experience, of no more value than wind that passes from the body. Now for the first time I had met the Self that is completely differentiated from sensual experience. It was a valuable discovery about my inner life that should not be lightly overlooked. It meant that I had come across the Self, the very fountainhead of my mind.

I must stress, however, that constant repetition of the experience was necessary, a thousand times, ten thousand times, a hundred thousand times, an uncountable number of times. By repeating our realization of the transcendental, pure consciousness, I came to realize that we must become liberated not only from external, sensory-based cognitive matters, but also from internal, mental images. I also came to understand through experience that I was in the "objectless concentration of mind," a state in which our whole being rests in peace and tranquillity. This I understood to be the "fourth stage of concentration" *(dhyāna)* that the Indian Buddhist philosopher Vasubandhu wrote about in his *Abhidharmakośavyākhyā.* I attained this state at the age of twenty-three, around the end of summer, and my enlightenment was acknowledged by Ueki Rōshi. I had long been perplexed by Kant's inclusion of the concept of "transcendental consciousness" within the framework of his philosophy, and I only gradually came to realize that it represented the influence of Vedic thought on his ideas. The *Vedas* speak of a realm of transcendental consciousness extending beyond sensory consciousness.

KEEP THIS IN MIND!

Do you watch your mind intently? There are, in fact, surprisingly few people who do. The mind is without shape or form, color or smell. It certainly has no weight. People do not, therefore, generally consider observing the mind itself objectively. Physical objects have a certain expanse, but the mind does not occupy any designated space. I remember reading in a psychology text by Professor Shinohara as a youth that the mind had only the function of "intent" ("intendieren"). Looking back now, I think the professor was probably influenced here by Husserl's phenomenology. Zen says, "The mind is shapeless and penetrates the ten directions." This seems to position the mind without adding the limitation of "intention." Husserl divided the mind itself into two poles—*noesis,* the process of perceiving, and *noema,* the object of perception—and attempted to elucidate the relationship between them. Having already touched on this subject earlier, I will not go any further into Kant's rebuttal of Hume's epistemology, as described in *A Treatise of Human Nature*. I would like, however, to comment that if we do not accept Hume's epistemology, we must accept Buddhist philosophy and its teaching that the mind represents the ultimate universal reality. Buddhism, and Zen in particular, places great stress on seeking out what the mind should be. Since the state of mind determines everything, it is hardly surprising that such attention should have been paid to it.

About seven hundred years ago there lived in Japan a great Zen priest named Myōchō, who is better known by his posthumous title, Kōzen Daitō Kokushi. He was a severe master, which is exemplified by the manner of his death. When close to death at the age of fifty-five and suffering from an injury to his left leg that prevented him from doing *zazen,* he broke his left knee in order to place his leg on his right thigh and died, bleeding, in the meditation posture. His blood-stained robe is kept at Daitokuji Temple in Kyoto to this day.

Myōchō is the author of a famous set of *Dying Admonitions,* which we used to chant at Unganji Temple during *zazen*. The first part of the *Admonitions* was compiled at a later time from excerpts of Myōchō's talks. It reads as follows: "You have all come to gather at this mountain [Daitokuji] for the sake of the Way, not for the sake of clothing or food. You have bodies which must be clothed, and you have mouths which must be fed. But what you must do, over and above that, is to confront that which you do not understand at every hour of the day and to seek after it without rest, whether you are coming or going. Time speeds away like an arrow; do not waste your time in frivolous thought. Keep this in mind!"

Keep what in mind? My opinion is that he meant what Husserl calls *noesis,* the mind's process of perceiving. *Noema,* the object of perception, has a multitude of appearances and is of no value in a serene search for mind. We should confront the workings of the mind itself and be able to reflect, "Ah, now I am getting excited," or "Now I am feeling greedy," or "Now I am deceiving myself with logic," or "I must judge myself objectivizing the functioning of the mind, and by doing so, purify and deepen my mind." What do you think?

CHOOSING YOUR DESTINY

Choices That Determine a Person's Destiny

At the end of my fourth year of elementary school I moved with my parents into the center of Kanuma, from Kamita-machi to Kamiyoko-machi. My father always saw the move as a great turning point in his life. Formerly a bedding merchant operating on the outskirts of the city, he had now moved into its center. He was filled with a great sense of achievement and success. Our new house was a row house like our former dwelling, but whereas we had had only two rooms before, we now had almost double that space on two floors. Directly opposite us was a radio shop, and next to it was a pharmacy specializing in women's medicines.

The pharmacist was one of our district's intellectuals. He often took me on his bike to go mushroom gathering on the hillside. I knew him for almost twenty-five years, from 1929 to 1953, and throughout that time he brought up time and time again the subject of his actions when he had worked for a large pharmaceutical maker. He never altered the prices of the products produced by the section he was responsible for, but maintained a low budget by lowering the quality of the ingredients employed. He was proud of the fact that he had won praise from his superiors for consistently attaining the designated profit.

The reason I have never forgotten this, though it happened more than sixty years ago, is that the story was a cause of great concern to me, young as I was, and that it still comes back to me. Why was my neighbor so proud of what appeared to me to be sheer deception, substituting inferior goods without the customers' knowledge? It took a long time and a great deal of experience for me to find an answer to this question. Is not the royal road to making a living giving the customer the best possible goods and services without his or her even being aware of it? If the customer does find out, he cannot help but be profoundly grateful. What is the psychological state of a person who could boast about doing the exact opposite? My conclusion was that people, in selecting their actions, do not do so on the basis of a cultivated value judgment. Many people disregard any value judgment at all and select a particular action more elliptically and instinctively. Moreover, few would think there is anything disgraceful about doing what he did. If the majority of people think like that, what is the best thing for us to do?

Most people live their lives selecting a constantly changing range of behavior. They do not treat their own behavior as the object of a cultivated value judgment. On the contrary, to do so would perhaps endanger their way of life. It is much like driving a car. The brake and the accelerator should not be operated after careful judgment but, rather, instinctively, without too much thought. The subconscious does not filter judgments, but selects what is practical. Thus, if we wish to act in the best possible way at all times, what should we do? We must plant in our subconscious a philosophy that provides a standard for producing proper behavior. This is a parting of the ways that determines a person's destiny. This standard is achieved through repeating the decisions reached through meditation. Zen considers all this to be a question of a person's environment and circumstances.

The pharmacist gradually sold less and less, and he and his family finally disappeared from Kanuma.

RUIN FROM A MOMENT'S MISTAKEN JUDGMENT

I recently read an article in a weekly magazine about a person who had resigned from the Tokyo District Public Prosecutor Office, where he was highly regarded as an excellent prosecutor, to enter private practice as a lawyer. As an auditor for a financial organization, he committed fraud and embezzlement and was jailed. There is a surprising number of such people in the world. This man had studied intensively to get into college, and then again to pass the extremely difficult judicial examination. He had made a future for himself in his field and then worked hard as a lawyer. Yet he ended up a criminal and was thrown into jail. In short, all his hard work was merely for the sake of becoming a criminal.

Whether you agree with my interpretation or not, there are certainly many people leading lives similar to his. How would you interpret this phenomenon?

Why should it happen that, in the mistaken judgment of a moment, all a person's efforts are nullified? Have you ever given this question serious consideration? Do you have biological knowledge that many different types of "mind," including that of God as well as that of the devil, have been transmitted to a person's subconscious? This is the state of a living human being. A life's work can be destroyed in an instant when a person is jailed. History is filled with such instances. What does it all mean? Why do such things happen? And given that they do happen, what can be done to rectify the situation? Despite the enormity of the issue, very few people regard it seriously and strive to solve it.

Biologically, all living beings preserve the total experience of their species in their individual bodies. We must realize just what a milestone this discovery was in modern biology, and the implications it holds. It is consequently a great mistake to think that our minds hold only our own experiences. Deep in our consciousness lie untold millennia of inherited consciousness of all the life that has gone before us. We must therefore understand that our state of mind is like a haunted house in which anything at all is capable of jumping out at us.

Two thousand five hundred years ago, the Buddha taught the Noble Eightfold Path: correct understanding, correct thought, correct speech, correct action, correct livelihood, correct effort, correct mindfulness, and correct concentration. These eight, he said, should be practiced as the virtues of daily life. A famous verse says: "Do no evil, do only good, purify your mind limitlessly: this is the teaching of the buddhas."

This teaching concerning the purification of the mind is, in my view, of enormously deep significance. To hold firmly to the attitude that we must at all times purify the mind limitlessly is to prevent catastrophe from falling upon us. A moment's carelessness obstructs the mind's purity and allows one's own demons to be called forth. We hear many stories of high government officials and prominent politicians being jailed; I do not think this results from any wish on their own part to become criminals. What occurs is a moment's inattention, a slackening of the reins of the mind, so that the deep-seated demons are allowed to pour forth. A life is destroyed because of the absence of a true philosophy (the study of living) in a person's existence.

COMPROMISE OR DESTRUCTION OF THE EGO?

Some people seek work on a self-employed basis, as lawyers, perhaps, or as public or tax accountants, while others make their living by being employed in large banks or corporations. In the latter case, the manner in which the connections between the employee and his or her employer are formed and constituted is a fundamentally important issue in the course of the employee's life. Those who prefer to be self-employed are vulnerable in that they must be constantly concerned with making money, for they would starve without clients. When they acquire greater stability, the acquisition of money is no longer such a pressing need, but because human beings tend to be creatures of habit, they find it quite difficult to escape from their former compulsion and tend to continue desiring money. Company employees, on the other hand, have the benefit of not having to face starvation (unless of course the company goes bankrupt); but they, in turn, must be constantly attentive to the relations between the company and themselves, and between themselves and their superiors and subordinates. This is an equally great burden.

I started out independently, first as a licensed tax accountant and then as a certified public accountant, and I was constantly exposed to the threat of starvation for the first five or six years, since I was forced to make my living in a harsh economic environment. Which path is best for any individual depends on his or her own personality and talents, and on a host of other factors. I consequently consider it a mistake to make a simple, clear-cut judgment concerning this question without considering these variables.

I have on my desk at the moment a book called *Problems of the Self* by Bernard Williams, a lecturer in philosophy at Cambridge University who has also taught at Oxford and Harvard and is a Fellow of the British Academy. In his book he takes up the subject of the human Self and discusses it from fifteen different angles. The first chapter is entitled "Personal Identity and Individuality" and the fifteenth "Egoism and Altruism." It is hardly surprising that, as a product of a Christian culture, he does not adopt the Buddhist perspective of the ultimate oneness of self and others. He does, however, advance from the conclusion that egoism is unethical in that he says, "If everyone were like him, he could not exist" (p. 252).

Considering how a person's ego should relate to the company he or she works for, I think there are two forms of modus vivendi: living according to a series of compromises, with constant adjustment between the desires of the individual and those of the company; or destroying the idea of the self so completely that the desires of the company become the desires of the self. Of course, the situation is different when the company's attitudes run fundamentally counter to the individual's sense of justice and view of how corporations should behave. When a firm is involved in fraudulent or corrupt activities, in particular, something we have been hearing a great deal about in the news recently, it is only natural that people of good conscience should refuse to be associated with such actions and that they should have no recourse but to quit as soon as possible and find a more worthwhile job.

Of the two choices, whether to compromise continually or to make the company part of one's ego, I think the second promises more advancement, since a person who lives in this way is greatly respected by the company. Nevertheless, he or she must then be able to surmount any difficulties resulting from conflicts with the ego thus abandoned.

I belong to the generation that remembers prewar society, the generation that was brought up to put social demands first and the self last. Fired by such slogans as, "We won't think of ourselves until we win (the war)," we would force our individual desires down and dream of serving our country to help it achieve victory. I do not, however, mean this kind of self-abasement when I talk about destroying the ego. That is of a completely different dimension.

Hakuin's master, Old Man Shōju, was a severe Zen teacher who lived in a small temple in what is now Iiyama (Nagano Prefecture) called Shōjuan, or Shōju's Hermitage. His own teacher had been Shidō Bunan, a former innkeeper at the way station of Sekigahara. His poem about the dew-drop reflecting the scarlet leaves of autumn, which I have already quoted above, reveals him to have been a man of utter transparency, reflecting the world about him as a dew-drop reflects whatever surface it occupies. Being transparent is what I mean by destroying the ego. The dewdrop is scarlet only because it rests on a scarlet leaf; in reality, it is a transparent drop of water unstained by the slightest speck of dust. Zen calls the state of transparency the state of mind of the enlightened person. When I recommend that you destroy the ego, I am speaking in a manner categorically different from the people who used to encourage us to forget our own needs and serve our country.

Destroying the ego is not the goal only of people leading a religious life, but it is the highest purpose in life for everybody. The philosopher Dr. Gustav Radbruch of Berlin University has said, for example, "One gains in personality by means of ego-forgetting objectivity" ("Zur Persönlichkeit wird man durch selbstvergessene Sachlichkeit"; *Rechtsphilosophie*, 8th ed., p. 149). Here, "personality" does not refer to the characteristics of a single person so much as to a perfected personality, an adept or master. The same idea appears in Hegel (*Phänomenologie des Geistes*, p. 413). In other words, whether in the East or the West, the highest way of living for a person is considered to be forgetting the self, the ego, completely and living life without the slightest stain on the mind. This is not a philosophy of self-sacrifice; it means, rather, using one's abilities with facility and freedom. I think any person who has attained this state, wherever he or she is, should be honored most, even in corporations.

How is it possible to live life with the ego destroyed? It is, in fact, the easiest of things; it only seems excessively difficult to those who do not understand it. It means to discover the Self that is without notion or concept, to experience and master it. When most people see the moon, a preconceived idea of it springs immediately to mind. When they see a mountain, the word "mountain" forms in their consciousness. All the same, it is possible to look at the moon or a mountain without forming any concept of them. It is possible to have concepts; it is equally possible not to have them. Strictly speaking, it takes an overwhelmingly long time to be able to live without forming impressions and conceptions regarding the objects of life. Zen expresses the spiritual phenomenon of living consciously without concepts phenomenologically through the koan of the "barrier." Those who live their lives unconsciously without conceptualizing the objects of life are very numerous. There is, however, a wide difference when it comes to those who do so consciously. It is surprising how simple this actually is, once it has been explained. Yet those who can practice it consciously are few and very accomplished; they live apart from notion and concept, experiencing the world directly. Nāgārjuna, the great Indian Buddhist philosopher, said that if we can experience this realm, we can throw off the body and roam freely through it. This is what it means to surmount any difficulties resulting from conflicts with the abandoned ego.

WHY COMPANY EMPLOYEES FAIL

There are four reasons behind people's failure in a company situation: First, they are thoroughly self-centered; second, they are absolute misers; third, they are completely lazy; or fourth, they take no notice of their surroundings or of other people.

The self-centered employee. What are you talking about, making the Self into nothing? We all like ourselves best, don't we? When the blocks are down, it's every man for himself! We should live for ourselves, from first to last. What's the point of pushing ourselves over something that won't profit us directly? We have to protect ourselves first in matters that can profit us, however important or unimportant. People might call us egocentric, but who cares about their criticism? I know it's right to be self-centered; what's the point of being neither one way nor the other, neither self-centered nor altruistic? Nobody can be punished for being self-centered. However much people might look down on people like us, the state is never going to execute us for our egocentricity. Consumer goods are all for our own benefit. Using the telephone for free is the same. However unjust some thing might be, if it isn't concerned with our own profit, we should just keep quiet and avoid getting involved.

The miserly employee. Haven't they always said that people who laugh over a cent will cry over a cent. We should take very good care not to use more money than we have to. We live in a monetary economy, and this means that, when all is said and done, money's the most important thing. Every cent counts. What about the old proverb, "Every pickle makes a nickle"? That's the way society is. It isn't a sin to want to save money rather than waste it on other people. On the contrary, hasn't making money been considered a virtue from ancient times? People may say behind our back that we're stingy, but they're wrong and are just bad-mouthing us. We don't have to take any notice of them. We don't mind smoking cigarettes and drinking coffee, as long as it doesn't go against our principle of saving our own money. After all, the founder of Matsushita Electric Industrial Company wasn't born wealthy. If you are worried about embarrassment or your reputation, you'll never be able to save money. You say it's important to throw yourself into everything you do. Well, we should throw ourselves into being misers.

The lazy employee. However hard I push myself, my company's never going to be number one in Japan or the world. However hard I work, my salary is never going to be a hundred times what it is now. All I want to do is live without attracting anyone's attention, without being late for work, and without getting too involved in my job. If I am noticed, I might find myself in a predicament, being given some kind of heavy responsibility I don't want and being forced to overexert myself. If I come in late, I'll also be noticed and perhaps find my job on the line. Whatever, I'm never going to advance all that much by working hard. So I'll just learn to pretend I've got my nose to the grindstone, and then I'll be all right. The objective is to lead a pleasant life as a salaried worker by being shrewd. Surely, you can't ask any more of life than to understand this and live in this way? Getting by without attracting anyone's attention, never being late, and not working too hard—that's my advice for any salaried worker. Stick to those three principles, and you'll be fine.

The arrogant employee. My family are descended directly from the Sun Goddess. I'm as different from you as a carrot from a turnip. I'm not interested in all the turnips around me; the social standing of their family is simply too different from mine. I haven't the slightest interest in anything about them. They're completely beneath my consideration. I only care about my own interests. Since I am living in this world, however, it is natural that the objects of interest will change at times. Still, I concentrate on them and ignore the rest. I don't suppose the president and the directors know how I feel. It's better that they don't. It's not all that easy to know what's inside a person's mind. I live my life heedless of the people and things around me. I believe that is the best way to live. Not that anyone's ever written about it, of course.

The above four types do not, of course, represent all the varieties of worker, but they are to be found in every workplace, and they will all, without doubt, fail in their careers. Sometimes, when only a paper's width divides two candidates, this will become the deciding factor. Not many people realize from what minute factors decisions are made.

ATTAINING TRUE INSIGHT

Some Thoughts on Attaining Intuitive Power

We all realize the necessity of intuitive power in our lives, but the problem is determining how to cultivate it. I doubt there is any school textbook that teaches us the best way to do so. I suppose no one writes textbooks about it because it would be a rather difficult topic to cover, given that it is not something that belongs to the objective realm. But does this mean that school textbooks tend to be concerned only with human knowledge and attaining the objects of that knowledge, and that they consequently discuss only those things that can be described objectively? Not necessarily. Textbooks are written in levels aimed at students with different abilities and different degrees of maturity. Even so, they tend to be written about what is objectively easy to understand. The contents may be more advanced or abstract, if this is considered necessary for the most highly skilled people. In this sense, the reason nothing is written in school texts about intuitive power is that there is no absolute standard for judging things that cannot be recorded factually and objectively.

This still leaves us with the question of what intuition is. Intuition means, I think, a power that does not need to employ any medium when one has some image or judgment. People tend to use words to represent their images. Law students learn to use the logic of syllogism, which is a classical method of using the medium of words to arrive at decisions. Intuition, on the other hand, does not use words as an expedient. Not only does it not use words as a medium for a judgment, but it does not employ expressions or images, either. It is an understanding of the essence of things, their direction and how they are likely to change, without relying on words or expressions. Thus, when we observe something functioning in a particular place and wonder what it is, we attempt to understand it by comprehending its present condition, observing the direction in which it is moving and grasping the significance of its tendency toward change through intuition, without using words or expressions as a medium. There is obviously more than one way of doing this. If we analyze all of the conditions of our environment comprehensively, for example, we should be able to understand them. Such an analysis would necessitate an almost infinite number of examinations, however, suggesting that, if the analysis lacks comprehensiveness, there is a real danger that misunderstandings might arise. It is in any event virtually beyond human ability to make such an analysis. Intuition, on the other hand, does not require the medium of words or expressions, and it is consequently direct, straightforward, and extremely quick. The question thus remains how we can make it work for us.

We have seen above how the sixth patriarch Hui-neng attained great enlightenment when his master, Hung-jen, spoke the words, "Raise [that] thought without letting it settle on any particular thing." Thus, the phrase "without letting [thought] settle on any particular thing" tells us we must not let our minds become attached to anything. "Raise [that] thought" begs the question of what kind of thought (expressed with the character for "mind" in the original) is meant. "That" suggests that a particular type of thought is being specified, though its nature is not, in fact, described. In other words, when the mind does not attach itself to anything, when it is not fixed, it is in a condition I would call the functioning of intuitive power. If we view it in this way, we can say that intuition is a spiritual power which human beings have always possessed. It includes the power of foresight, but it has nothing to do with the fluent use of words or with speculative thinking. Rather, it is a function and an operation that has human spirituality as a direct foundation. There is, however, no need to say as a consequence that the limitless stock of experiences and knowledge stored in the subconscious and the deep consciousness is useless. We should rather see intuition as something which functions while maintaining this rich store below the surface of consciousness. Intuitive power is cultivated by tempering the mind so perfectly that it remains attached to nothing.

ACQUIRING THE POWER OF INSIGHT

It is beyond question that the thing people living in this world need most to acquire is the power of insight. This is nowhere more obvious than in the workplace, where a demonstration of insight with respect to the nature and direction of various matters is essential. We have only to think how important it is to be able to read the actions of colleagues, understand the personalities of those in management positions, judge how our own assignment is advancing, and discern movements in the national economy.

In his book *Executive Decision Making,* Dr. Jones, a professor at Illinois University, lists the power of discernment as the most important of four factors governing the advancement of one employee over the rest of the work force (p. 169). In this connection I remember a book that impressed me greatly as a youth, *Montgomery's Auditing.* Here, too, "intuition" is mentioned as absolutely necessary for a successful auditor (8th ed., p. 17). Hegel, too, in his *Phänomenologie des Geistes* (Phenomenology of the Spirit), spoke of the absolute importance of "pure insight" ("die reine Einsicht"). The necessity of insight is therefore widely attested. How, though, can it be attained?

None of the above writers who commend insight or intuition actually explains how to acquire it. The words "in-sight" and "intuition" do not explain it either. People may understand the words themselves, but they do not know how to attain what they signify. But this is not to say that they themselves have not experienced intuition and insight, how-ever faintly or obscurely. Surely, however dim or hesitant the experience, they must have realized at certain times, "This is intuition," or "I've shown insight here." What they have not experienced is the inquiry or search after such things within the patterns of daily life such as to enable intuition to be employed at will on the surface of life. How, then, do we go about examining it? Let us hear the Buddha's views on the subject. His direct teachings are contained in scriptures known in Sanskrit as the *Āgamas* and in Pali as the *Nikāyas*. The Japanese were late in realizing the vital importance of these sutras and did not really become familiar with them until the end of the nineteenth century. This was because Chih-i (538–597), the founder of T'ien-t'ai (Tendai) Bud-dhism in China, devised a method known as "the five periods and the eight teachings" for classifying the enormous mass of Buddhist writings and teachings that had been translated into Chinese. Explaining that the Buddha taught in five dis-tinct periods between the age of thirty-five, when he attained enlightenment, and the age of eighty, when he died, Chih-i assigned all the translated sutras to one or another of these periods. The *Āgamas* were placed in the second period, be-ginning three weeks after the enlightenment and lasting twelve years, intimating that they were inferior to the rounded, mature teaching of his final period, the *Lotus Sutra*. Buddhists in China, Korea, and Japan consequently took little notice of them. A number of Chinese priests developed similar schemes in a process generally referred to as "dividing the periods of the teachings" *(p'an-chiao)*, usually for the purpose of proving that the sutras most favored by their sect contained the most complete truth. Such classification and organization are features of Chinese Buddhism, necessitated by the Chinese translations of Buddhist writings in an order completely unrelated to the time of their composition. The great thirteenth-century Japanese Buddhist, Nichiren, produced a similar scheme to prove that the *Lotus Sutra* was the Buddha's final teaching. In actual fact, of course, modern scholarship has shown that the *Lotus Sutra* was composed four hundred years after the Buddha's death.

An important passage in the *Āgamas* states that there are various fields or realms belonging to the objects of cognition, including the eyes, ears, nose, tongue, tactile body, and mental consciousness. Contact with them gives rise to form (material objects), feeling (sensations), perception (representations or ideas), mental constituents (volition), and consciousness. They are all considered to be impermanent, suffering, lacking in self, and subject to cessation. "These are not ours," said the Buddha. This is significant, for it means that the five elements or "aggregates" of which all beings are composed (form, feeling, perception, mental constituents and consciousness) are not the "True Self." Thus, the Buddha taught, "These are not yours [Pali *natumhāka*]," and he recommended that we cast them away. Once we abandon the five aggregates, we live in the True Self alone, and we attain the six superhuman powers of the Buddha. True insight comes when these six powers are attained; or, that is, when enlightenment is attained.

TOWARD INSIGHT

The *Dhammapada* is an ancient Indian Buddhist work. My copy contains both the Pali original and an English translation and commentary by the great Indian philosopher and former president of the republic, Sarvepalli Radhakrishnan (Oxford University Press, 1984 [8th ed.]). The work is made up of twenty-six short chapters. The twentieth, entitled "The Path" *(Maggavaggo),* contains seventeen short verses, in which are found a number of particularly important passages.

The first verse contains the words, "Of virtues, freedom from attachment is the best." The Buddha's words are reminiscent of the freedom and enlightenment attained by Hui-neng on hearing the words from the *Diamond Sutra,* "Raise [that] thought without letting it settle on any particular thing." In the second verse we find the statement, "This is the path, there is none other that leads to the purifying of insight." Insight is usually thought to have many stages, but there is only one path which leads to the highest and purest form of it. This is the path characterized by perfect liberation from all attachment. This is simple to conceptualize but extremely difficult to attain in practice. Realizing freedom from attachment to the thoughts that come and go requires considerable training. This is probably the reason so much importance is attached to religious training following enlightenment.

The *Dhammapada* employs the expression "purification of insight"; Hegel's "pure insight," I think, is extremely similar. In his *Phenomenology of the Spirit* he judges the "power of pure insight" to be the highest form of learning.

Since it involves a constant state of "no-thought," it is not surprising that it should take considerable training to achieve. As that training advances, the matter of one's destination becomes reflected, without effort, in the subject. To my mind, the power of pure insight is the same as the superhuman ability to see everything others cannot, one of the six powers of the Buddha mentioned in the *Lotus Sutra*. It also includes another of them, of course, insight into the mind of others.

Ueki Rōshi died, as he had predicted, on May 26, 1967, when the tree peonies were in full bloom. The day after his private funeral, I had the opportunity to ask his successor, Tetsuzen Watanabe Rōshi, in a room on the west side of the main hall of the temple, what he had valued the most in our late master. Watanabe Rōshi replied, "His function." "Function" is a term used in Zen temples to describe the power people have to function well. As Watanabe elaborated, "When we were trainee priests, Ueki Rōshi would gather us together and say, 'Do you realize I passed through your very being two or three times a day wearing clogs with high supports?' " Ueki Rōshi knew the inner self of each and every one of his disciples. This was possible only because the Rōshi had polished his "purity of insight" over and over again. I agree with Watanabe's statement, "This, I think, was the greatest thing about Ueki Rōshi."

The Buddha spoke in many ways about attaining purity of mind. He warns us in the *Dhammapada*, "You yourself must strive," and "Who is weak in resolution and thought, that lazy and idle man will not find the way to wisdom" ("The Path," verses 4 and 8).

TWO NECESSARY CONDITIONS FOR ATTAINING INSIGHT

Two things are necessary on the path to acquiring insight. The first is to experience with the full force of your being that the essence of all human existence, both your own and others', is emptiness. Since the idea of experiencing this from scratch is very puzzling, let us consider for a moment the seventh case recorded in the *Blue Cliff Record*, "What is one phrase of the pre-voice [absolute reality]?" or, "What was your face before your mother and father were born? Where were you before your parents were born?" We can explain this logically. Since you are here now, it stands to reason you must have been somewhere in the universe before your parents were born. Nothing is produced from an absolute vacuum. Where you were and in what form is open to question, but it is absolutely certain that you were born of your parents, as they were born of theirs. Counting back thirty-five generations, to around the time of the Magna Carta, your ancestors number over 17,100,000,000. Counting back fifty generations to the time of Charlemagne, your ancestors total 560,332,800,000,000. A mere three generations still earlier, the number soars to over 4,480,000,000,000,000. These calculations assume that each ancestor produced at least one child by the age of twenty-five. These enormous figures highlight the never-ending cycle of birth and death of your ancestors, which has led eventually to your own life, and give meaning to the life that you have inherited. You must have been somewhere there among your ancestors. Our origin, our very essence, lies in absolute emptiness (not an absolute physical vacuum) in which there is neither shape nor form, color nor smell. Two thousand five hundred years ago in the forests of northern India, the Buddha came to the realization that the essence of self is emptiness. This idea of emptiness, so fundamental to Buddhism, was the result of the Buddha's intense meditation. Simply to know that our being is emptiness, however, is like reading about it in a newspaper. We have to verify the truth of the statement with every cell of our body, renewing that experience time and time again through meditation so that it is accepted physically as well as mentally. When we can do so, our consciousness of ego necessarily melts away. The absence of ego means that the mind is constantly at one with the universe. Since the mind is without form, there remains nothing that can sense even that "I am the universe." There is no "I."

The second thing necessary on the path to acquiring insight is training to ensure that two thoughts do not string themselves together. Most people's lives are spent on a constant journey of the consciousness. It goes from place to place, so that we live, as it were, in the stream of consciousness. As we have seen above, however, this condition of mind breeds residual patterns (paribhāvana), habits of thought that have stained the mind. Unless we undertake strenuous training to eliminate them, they will take root. To stop this happening, we must be sure that we do not allow trains of thought to arise. Each thought must be allowed to enter and leave the mind without starting a train in its wake. This is not difficult to accomplish if we are able to experience complete emptiness. When we have reached this stage, we must take it a step further to prevent even the initial thought from arising. Wu-hsüeh Tsu-yüan (1226–1286), the Chinese priest who was Zen master to Hōjō Tokimune, the de facto ruler of Japan, left a verse on his death which said:

Coming, nothing goes forward;
Going, nothing retreats.

Though a person appears before him, he has no awareness in his mind that someone has come, and similarly, when a person departs, he does not think, "Ah, I am seeing him off." As such training accumulates, we realize for ourselves that, mystery upon mystery, we have attained intuitive power. The Buddha, though, cautioned his disciples against undergoing training merely to acquire such powers.

THE SHORTEST ROUTE TO ATTAINING INSIGHT

Mircea Eliade writes in *Yoga: Immortality and Freedom* (Princeton University Press, 1971), "The Buddha did not encourage his disciples to seek *siddhis*. The one true problem was deliverance, and the possession of 'miraculous powers' entailed the danger that it might turn the monk away from his original goal, nirvana." This is a very important point. The way to enlightenment is also the path by which superhuman powers are obtained. Though such powers appear naturally at a certain stage, the Buddha warned his followers not to practice with the objective of acquiring them, since such a purpose is at odds with the determination to seek enlightenment. Purifying the subconscious to bring it into complete unity with the surface consciousness is a vital first step on the path to enlightenment. The result is similar, since superhuman powers are naturally acquired anyway with enlightenment, but this does not mean they should be sought as the objective of training.

Although a fondness for misunderstanding seems to be a human attribute, the Buddha's followers had a tendency to want to confuse the means and the ends and to practice with the intention of attaining the supernatural power acquired by an enlightened person. Thus, the Buddha seems to have taken the attitude that it is better not to encourage the uniform attainment of supernatural powers as the purpose of liberation, in order to prevent his disciples from stepping onto a wrong path. This is a subtle, but very important, point. Money is a sine qua non in modern society, yet a person whose sole purpose in life is to acquire it is making a big mistake. Such extreme attitudes lead to warped people like the hotel owner who was reluctant for economic reasons to install the required fire detection equipment in his hotel, with the result that when a fire broke out, more than thirty people died in the conflagration.

When a person attains the spiritual state of nirvana, otherwise known as enlightenment, he has also reached the point at which he gains insight automatically. Zen Master Bassui (1327–1387) wrote, "Seeing into one's own nature *[kenshō]* is in itself the six powers." When a person "sees into his own nature" (that is, becomes enlightened), he also gains the six supernatural powers (two of which, the ability to see into the heart of things and the ability to know the mind of others, can be considered to comprise "insight"). This is not to say, however, that everyone who has had his or her enlightenment confirmed possesses the same degree of insight. As Bassui says, "Though the Dharma is said to be one, not two, enlightenment may be shallow or deep, and there are differences in the styles of teaching." As a result, the degree of insight differs with the depth of enlightenment. In the same way, there was a world of difference between Ueki Rōshi and his successor, Watanabe Rōshi.

The quickest way to attain enlightenment is through meditation. Buddhism calls this meditation Zen, from the Sanskrit word of the same meaning, *dhyāna*. There are various degrees of attainment within meditation, just as there are licensed tax accountants of varying abilities. Around the year 300 there lived in present-day Afghanistan three brothers, Asaṅga, Vasubandhu, and Viliñcivatsa, all of whom grew up to be great Buddhist philosophers. Vasubandhu wrote a voluminous treatise called the *Abhidharmakovśavyākhyā*, which is known today through the original Sanskrit and through the Chinese translation of Hsüan-tsang. In it he divides meditation into four stages, likening the fourth to the absolutely steady flame of a candle in a tightly sealed room. The superior form of insight is that which emerges from the acquisition of such an immovable mind.

GOING BEYOND INSIGHT

Vasubandhu considered the fourth stage of Zen described above as the superior form. A certain amount of resolution and effort is needed to attain it. Such effort is necessary because most people are generally caught up in the things of the external world and do not particularly concern themselves with seeking their own truth.

When I was at university I attended hardly any lectures more than the once necessary to fulfill the minimum requirement. By the time I graduated, I had not spent more than two weeks in the classroom. I found that the lecturers were too concerned with subtleties of theory regarding the objective world, and I judged them to be nothing more than tradesmen in academia. This disappointed me greatly, and so

I quit going to school. Today, I am not sure whether that decision was good or bad. As far as I was concerned at the time, however, education, especially in the humanities, was concerned with human beings, and any theoretical structure must therefore necessarily be based on how human beings were understood. If this fundamental issue is ignored, the meaning of education is turned around, such that it becomes the mere pursuit of the systematized minutiae of various subjects concerned with the objects of the physical world. I had no interest in wasting my youth in classes taught by people who thought that way. I decided it would be far more worthwhile to educate myself by reading one hundred pages of original foreign language text and two hundred pages of Japanese literature a day.

I have before me a book called *Karl Engisch, Beiträge zur Rechtstheorie* (Karl Engisch: His Contributions to the Theory of Law), published in 1984 in Frankfurt-am-Main and written by various scholars of legal theory. In reading it, I was greatly surprised by the large number of names of philosophers and legal scholars mentioned: Kant, Heinrich Rickert, Bernhard Bolzano, Rudolf Stammler, Hans Kelsen, Gustav Lambert Radbruch, and Georg Jellinek, not to mention Plato and Aristotle. Obviously, the contributors, all legal scholars, are interested in first establishing the nature of man as a basis for discussing legal theory. Such an approach is absolutely necessary; there is no value in education that is concerned from first to last simply with interpreting the meanings of phrases and words in legal texts. My criticism is not limited to law studies, either. Nicklisch's famous *Die Betriebswirtschaft* (Economics) also begins with an examination of the essential qualities of human beings (p. 16). Such an attitude among scholars is of decisive importance. In this sense, it is very much open to doubt whether many Japanese academics are true scholars or merely tradesmen in learning. I have heard it reported by someone in the same school that a certain prominent university professor complained openly that "Iizuka spends two pages criticizing me in his thesis. What right has he got to be awarded a doctorate?" This is a typical case of mixing the public with the private.

I have digressed. To return to my original topic, I believe that the most important aspect of the search for self is the relentless pursuit of the answer to the question, "What is my original essence?" This is what the Buddha termed "emptiness." The Buddhist emptiness has nothing to do with the absolute vacuum of physics, or the negation of nihilism. It is merely the term applied to the original absence of any distinguishing form, such as shape, color, or smell. The truth of the teaching of emptiness must be verified in every pore of the body and in every recess of the mind. It has no power, however, if it is comprehended only as an idea. Having thus verified emptiness, the next step is to break down the barrier constructed from the large boulders of mental habits. In fact, unless we do so, we will be unable to achieve a true understanding of emptiness. Human beings store untold millions of mental experiences in their minds, from the time they begin to take notice of their surroundings until they reach adulthood. At some time, these experiences harden into fixed mental habits and create a false sense of self. Because of the enormous obstruction they cause, most people are unable to come into contact with their true Self.

THREE CONDITIONS FOR LIVING THE HIGHEST FORM OF LIFE

According to Radhakrishnan (*Indian Philosophy*, vol. 1, p. 432), the Buddha repeatedly identified three conditions as necessary for living the highest form of human life. The three, in no particular order of importance, are faith, insight, and cultivation of the mind.

It is of course not sufficient to believe in just anything, such as a sardine's head. Faith comes from observing something as absolutely correct. There is, for example, a scroll hanging in the alcove of the master's room in the meditation hall of Myōshinji Temple in Kyoto which reads, "Train hard, and the resulting illumination will be vast." In other words, have faith in the way of life you are following. Such faith is not at all common, however, for there are so many people wandering about in delusion. In the thirty-two years I trained under Ueki Rōshi, two ordained priests fled from the temple, losing their way in the strictness of the practice there.

One day as I was sitting beside a brazier with Ueki Rōshi, I questioned him on this subject. "Rōshi, I have a question," I began. "There are tens of thousands of Buddhist priests in Japan. How many of them do you think have committed themselves to becoming great Zen masters?" The Rōshi replied, "One hair on nine cows." The number of hairs in the coats of nine cows must be vast, yet the Rōshi considered that a true practitioner of Zen was like just one hair shared by all nine. Only one among millions possesses true faith, and it is not easy to maintain such faith, either.

It is the same with insight. Very few people possess it, which means that people who successfully penetrate the truth of human life are rare indeed. Most are not interested in polishing their intuitive power. If they think about it a bit, it is only spasmodically; almost no one attempts seriously to polish the power of insight with which we are naturally endowed. This is the problem. Since relatively few people consider themselves seriously, insight and other spiritual and mental qualities are little in evidence. This tendency can only be expected to increase in the future. Most people do not attempt to observe the essence of their mind, living instead attached to the mind's objects.

Those who practice cultivation of the mind are, likewise, few and far between. "To cultivate the mind" means to train it incessantly so that it attaches itself to nothing. Zen masters often use the phrase "a hundred polishings, a thousand forgings," stressing that the cultivation of the mind cannot be carried out half-heartedly. Thousands and even millions of repetitions are necessary. We saw in the previous chapter that Kūkai, when he was eighteen, met a Buddhist priest who recommended he read the sutra called the *Kōkūzō gumonji no hō* (Ākāśagarbha Bodhisattva's power-filled, wish-fulfilling, supreme mind mantra technique for seeking hearing and retention). Training according to its ritual methods allowed him to polish his natural genius through a million repetitions, without stops and starts, of the *dhāranī* (a Sanskrit phrase calling on the powers of the deity) set out in the sutra. This was a truly demanding rite. The anguish he experienced is suggested by his confession in the *Collected Works of Prose and Poetry of Kūkai* that he lost his direction many times and wept. What is certain is his attitude toward his training, which he undertook at the risk of life itself. Through cultivation, the mind becomes focused and free from the distraction of thought, and the practitioner, through thorough polishing of his mind, gains superhuman powers. *The Ten Stages of the Development of Mind*, which Kūkai wrote when he was sixty, contains quotations from more than six hundred Chinese sources. This was at a time, it must be remembered, when there were no pens or notebooks to facilitate writing, so he must have recalled them from memory. All the same, such powers are inherent in all human beings.

CULTIVATING THE MIND

Let us look a little more deeply into the three conditions mentioned in the previous section. The first thing I would like to stress is that very few people look into their own mind. Though many might think they do, and would declare that they know their own mind best, it is in fact only a very few particularly accomplished people who actually do so. This is because most people do not consciously try to train themselves not to string two thoughts together, as recommended by the Zen master Hakuin and the Chinese master Chu-hung. The irony is that ordinary, ignorant people such as ourselves actually live all the time without stringing thoughts together; the only problem is that we do not realize it. Eating, for example, is for most of us a daily activity. We do not think consciously that we should stretch our hands out to pick up our knife and fork, or voice the concept of food in our mind. It is the same when we drink our soup: we do not keep every action this entails on the surface of our mind. In this sense, we spend a large portion of our life not stringing thoughts together.

You might think it does not matter whether or not we consciously experience not stringing two thoughts together. In fact, it does matter, because most people already do not do so without being aware of it. Since they lack all consciousness of not doing so, however, they also lack all sense of discovery (or in other words, enlightenment). They do not know that not stringing two thoughts together is the ultimate reality of their lives. Not knowing, they simply live without doing it. There is a boundless difference between realizing and not realizing, a hundred thousand mile gulf.

As we live consciously without stringing two thoughts together and training ourselves to attain that objective, our minds gradually become increasingly transparent. For the slightest instant, it appears as if we can actually grasp the workings of our mind. What Zen calls "enlightenment" can be thought of as a synonym for "self-realization." It is the condition of being able to understand the slightest pin-prick of change in the mind. Since the mind is so open, we see its movements in perfect clarity: "Ah, I'm talking out of selfishness," "Ah, now I'm about to act out of anger," "Ah, jealously has overcome my judgment." When we can thus see into our own mind, the strange thing is that we can also see into the minds of others. This Buddhism calls "the superhuman power to see into the mind of others."

Most people never reach this stage, because they never consciously train themselves to live without stringing thoughts together. In other words, they do not "train hard." They live naturally not stringing thoughts together, but, being unconscious of it, are not aware when they become captive to their egocentricity or slaves to their desires, or when they turn into demons of jealousy. This, unfortunately, is how the majority of people today live. They are to be pitied. Long ago, a great Chinese Zen master called Ta-hui confessed honestly that he had achieved great enlightenment eighteen times and lesser enlightenment countless times. As ignorant ordinary mortals grow and mature, we accumulate something on the order of an infinite number of enlightenments, discoveries, and self-realizations. It is very rare to achieve enlightenment suddenly overnight as Hui-neng did; the majority of people move to higher levels of enlightenment through a nearly countless series of discoveries and insights. It costs not a cent to train oneself not to string thoughts together, so you would think more people would try it. Lost in the stream of their fixed mental habits, however, they neglect this training.

4

The Wisdom of the Buddha

RAISE THOUGHT WITHOUT LETTING IT SETTLE ON ANY PARTICULAR THING

Chinese Zen speaks of six patriarchs: Bodhidharma, who brought the teachings to China from India, Hui-k'o (487–593), Chien-chih (d. 606), Tao-hsin (580–651), Hung-jen (601–674), and Hui-neng (638–713). Why Hui-neng is generally considered to have been the man who brought Chinese Zen to completion I do not know. I suppose it is because Hui-neng appears to have been the first to speak of Zen in a way ordinary people could understand and the popularizer of the expression "seeing into one's own nature" (*kenshō* in Japanese).

This expression poses many problems. It is used in Zen to mean enlightenment. Enlightenment is generally, though mistakenly, thought to be very difficult to attain, necessitating long years of training. We have the example of Anbara Heishirō, however, a carpenter, who, having heard Zen Master Hakuin lecturing in the next room, shut himself up in the bathroom to meditate and attained enlightenment overnight. Zen is in no way connected with whether a person is learned or not, his or her scholastic attainments, or how long he or she has trained. All that is necessary is that a person see into the essence of his or her own mind through a concentration of the spirit. This "seeing into" is, of course, no shallow action such as peeping at something. Zen Master Bassui spoke of it as "penetrating one's mind." Unless people bring their penetrating insight to life through training, like taking an object in the hand, it cannot be *kenshō*.

Recently, however, the expression has been used far too broadly, and care is consequently needed. I place the blame for this at Hakuin's door. There is a general tendency to refer to the first stage attained after beginning Zen practice as *kenshō*, which is vastly different in meaning from Hui-neng's usage. Hui-neng, who lived in the seventh century during the T'ang dynasty in China, was reputedly illiterate, with no experience in Zen training. He described himself as a farmer from Ling-nan, in the present-day province of Kuang-tung. His father was an exile who died an early death. Hui-neng supported his mother and himself by cutting firewood in the hills and selling it in the marketplace. Being illiterate, he lived in the direst poverty. One day, a customer bought firewood from him and asked him to deliver it to his house. As he was leaving, he noticed a priest standing in the doorway reciting the *Diamond Sutra*. "Where are you from, and what sutra are you reading?" he asked. He learned that the priest was from Tung-shan Temple on Mount Huang-mei in the province of Hu-pei and that the fifth patriarch Hung-jen was at present residing there, giving lectures on the *Diamond Sutra* in the company of more than a thousand disciples. Hui-neng begged ten pieces of silver for the support of his old mother and set off for Mount Huang-mei to see Hui-jeng.

When he saw Hui-neng, Hung-jen asked, "Where do you come from, and what are you seeking?" "I am a farmer from Ling-nang and I seek to become a buddha," replied Hui-neng. Hung-jen then commented insultingly, "A man from Ling-nan? How can a man from a place of exile like that ever become a buddha?" Hui-neng answered, "A man may come from the north or the south, but the buddha-nature knows no north or south. What discrimination can there be in the buddha-nature?" Hung-jen realized then that this was no ordinary man. All the same, he brushed him off, ordering him away to work in a shed at the back of the temple, cutting wood and pounding rice. And there Hui-neng stayed for the next eight months. Although Hui-neng was lame, he managed to do his job, which necessitated pounding rice with his feet.

One day, Hung-jen posed a question for his disciples concerning life and death. This resulted in a dispute between Hui-neng and Shen-hsiu, who had already studied under the master for six years. They both composed verses concerning their understanding. Hung-jen considered Shen-hsiu's understanding still to fall short of true penetration of his own nature. In the meantime, Hui-neng had asked someone to write his own verse upon the wall. When Hung-jen saw it, he called Hui-neng to his room in the depths of the night and lectured to him on the *Diamond Sutra*. It was when he uttered the words "Raise thought without letting it settle on any particular thing" that Hui-neng attained great enlightenment. This story is found in the *Platform Sutra of the Sixth Patriarch*.

HUI-NENG, THE SIXTH PATRIARCH

Hung-jen asked his disciples to compose verses showing their understanding of their own mind. The Fifth Patriarch considered that, of all the various questions of human life, that concerning life and death was the most important. His disciples did not strive to solve the question in a personal sense, however, but concerned themselves only with the Three Treasures (the Buddha, the Dharma, and the Samgha) and with making food offerings to the spirits of the dead or chanting sutras for their sake and for the merits of doing this. That is to say, they hoped only to achieve virtue through their actions.

Shen-hsiu, the leading disciple and a fine priest, wrote in the middle of the night the following verse on the wall outside the master's room as an expression of his own understanding:

The body is the Bodhi tree [the tree of enlightenment].
The mind is the stand of a bright mirror.
Wipe it constantly with diligence,
So that it remains unstained by dust.

The verse was useless as an expression of enlightenment, but Hung-jen called his disciples to him all the same and lit incense before the verse, praising it and urging them to memorize it, for if they were to observe it in their practice they

Śrāvastī. At that time the World-honored One addressed the bhik-śus saying, "Bhikśus, you should understand that form is impermanent. Those who regard it that way are considered to have a correct view of it.

This was the Buddha's first teaching. Form *(rūpa)* is a term used in Buddhist writings to describe material stimulation from the outside world. Shapes and colors seen by the eye, voices and sounds heard by the ear, smells sensed by the nose, have come into being, like flowing water, through causes and conditions and therefore have no permanent, unchanging nature. This, the Buddha said, is how we should regard all objects in the material realm.

This is a crucially important passage. Like Kant's epistemology, it touches on the principles of human knowledge. We experience the outside world by receiving various stimulations through our eyes, ears, nose, tactile body, and tongue. The images we form from these stimulations we consider to constitute a true picture of the outer world. This view is shared by the epistemology of David Hume, who said we receive impressions of all that which is outside ourselves through the medium of our senses. This is perhaps the most sensible theory of the origins of knowledge. Kant, however, smashed it head-on, saying that human beings have absolutely no knowledge of what is outside themselves. Stimulation from objects in the outer world are received by the senses and constructed there as well. Only knowledge of things is formed (Kant's *Prolegomena*). This is Kant's mistake. The Buddha spoke about the fundamental construction that gives rise to human knowledge far earlier. All the various phenomena of the outer world that human sensations

would certainly not fall by the wayside. It was a tremendous acknowledgment. Hung-jen may have been concerned for his own safety, remembering that Bodhidharma was reputed to have been poisoned by jealous rivals. In the middle of the night, however, the Patriarch called Shen-hsiu to his room and said to him, "This verse you have composed reveals that you have not yet perceived your self-nature. You have arrived at the threshold of enlightenment, but you have not yet entered it. Write your verse again and submit it."

A few days later, a young novice happened to pass by the place where Hui-neng was pounding rice, chanting Shen-hsiu's verse aloud. Hui-neng knew immediately that it could not have been written by a person who had realized his own self-nature. He had the youth take him to where the verse was pinned up, and because he could not read, had him read it for him. Hui-neng then asked a priest called Chang Jih-yung to write a verse he had composed himself upon the wall for him. It read:

Enlightenment has not a tree from the beginning.
The bright mirror is not a stand.
Since originally there is nothing,
How could it be stained by dust?

When the priests in the temple saw the verse, they were astounded. Hung-jen, hearing the commotion and looking to see what the excitement was about, saw the verse. Fearing that someone would try to kill Hui-neng, and concerned that then there would be no one to succeed him, he camouflaged his true feelings and said to his assembled disciples, "This verse, too, has not yet perceived self-nature. Why on earth are you praising it?" The Fifth Patriarch was obviously very tense. So worried was he about protecting his chosen successor, he did not hesitate to deceive his followers.

Hui-neng's "How could it be stained by dust?" is like a verse by the retired emperor Hanazono (1297–1348), which reads in part: "Not a speck of dust marked the great earth." If we look at things physically, dust is piled high, and it is sophistry to say there is nothing. These verses do not speak of the physical, however, but point instead directly to the realm of enlightenment. In much the same way the Chinese Zen priest Wu-hsüeh Tsu-yüan, threatened with death by Mongol soldiers who had broken into his temple, wrote:

In all of heaven and earth
There's no room
Even to stand a stick upright.

Considered physically and spatially, this is strange. We should understand it, rather, to express a mind dwelling in emptiness which attaches to nothing.

THE ĀGAMAS

I remember that one of the questions on the entrance examination I took for the Law Department of Tōhoku Imperial University in March 1939 concerned the Buddhist council held to collect the teachings of the Buddha. Only eleven of the 386 candidates were accepted into the faculty of law and literature, and of these, a mere five received permission to study in the Law Department. The examination itself was, as you can imagine, rigorous.

After the Buddha's death more than 2,500 years ago some of the less dedicated of his disciples felt relief that they

would no longer have to submit to his severe discipline. The Venerable Kāśyapa, fearing that the teachings might fall into ruin, selected five hundred of the disciples, gathered them together in a cave and had them listen as Ānanda recited all that he had heard the Buddha teach or had memorized from earlier teachings. The disciples, in turn, memorized what Ānanda recited, and this formed the basis of what we know today as the *Āgama Sutras*. Legend adds that later councils were held to verify that what had been memorized was correct. This is, in essence, the answer I wrote in my examination paper. Buddhism has a vast number of volumes of sacred works, but what the Buddha actually taught can be found only in the *Āgamas*.

I later came into possession of *Some Sayings of the Buddha,* a book by Professor F. L. Woodward published by Oxford University Press. A truly fine work, it is an English translation of part of the Pali Canon. For me, reading it was a reconfirmation of the fundamental experience in my search into the nature of human life that I had begun at the age of sixteen with my study of Zen. Woodward's summary of the teachings of the *Āgamas (Nikāyas)* is also valuable in that scholars estimate the *Āgamas* to contain 17,505 sutras, and it would require considerable effort to read them all through. The fact that the modern Japanese translation of the *Āgamas* (made up of four groups of sutras) begins with the *Tso-a-han ching,* the Chinese translation of the *Saṁsyuktāgama,* shows how important the sutras in this particular grouping are considered to be. Let me give an example from this work:

Thus have I heard. On one occasion the Buddha was staying in Jeta Grove [Jetavana Monastery], the garden of Anāthapiṇḍika,

form are in constant flux; they are not permanent or un-changing. A wooden plaque hangs under the eaves on the southern side of the main hall of Unganji Temple in Nasu. It reads:

Where does your face go [after death]?
I do not know.
Only the peach blossoms blow in the spring wind,
This year, just as last.

The *Āgama Sutras* teach that this truth is the very heart of Buddhist philosophy.

BANKEI

Bankei Yōtaku (1622–1693) was a Zen priest who was born in what is now Himeji in Hyōgo Prefecture. His father was a masterless samurai from Shikoku who died when Bankei was ten. His mother lived, however, to the age of ninety-one, dying when Bankei was fifty-eight. His first spiritual uncertainty was generated by a phrase in the *Great Learning*, one of the four books of Chinese Confucianism: "The Way of Great Learning consists in manifesting bright virtue." What was this "bright virtue," he wondered. He consequently traveled from scholar to scholar to gain elucidation, but he met with no success. This had occurred when he was around fifteen, an age when people first begin to awaken to the fundamental questions of human life. The passion of Bankei's quest astonishes me. He was told by a Zen priest that if he wanted to find an answer to his question, he should do Zen meditation *(zazen)*. As a result, "he immediately commenced meditation. He went upon a nearby mountain, eating nothing for seven days, and there, on a massive crag, spread out his clothes on a rock and took up the correct position for *zazen*. He did not care whether he lost his life, and he did not rise from his seat until he naturally fell down. If someone had not brought him food, he would not have eaten" (*Hōgoshū*, p. 176).

Still, he could find no answer. He visited senior priests in many places, but he did not take to any of them. According to the *Gyōgōkyokki* (Account of the Deeds [of Zen Master Bankei), compiled by Sandō Chijō, he would cry out in his distress, reminding us of how Kūkai "cried many a time standing at the crossroads." This gives us a clear idea of Bankei's distress and his willingness to throw his life away for the sake of his religious training. When he was around twenty-four he "built a small ten-foot square hut and stopped up all the walls, allowing only food to be passed in and bowls to be collected through a small opening in one of the walls. He built a privy against one of the walls, and used it from within" (*Hōgoshū*, p. 179). This description testifies to the extent to which he gambled with his life in his burning quest.

During this time Bankei fell very ill. He "then became sicker and sicker. His body weakened. When he vomited, the bloody phlegms hardened and rolled in globules large as a thumb-tip. Once when he had vomited on the wall, he saw the globules rolling down one after the other" (p. 180). Only thin rice gruel would pass down his throat, and the young Bankei thought that he was approaching death. Truly unconcerned by this realization, he gained enlightenment. He confessed, "Just then, spontaneously, I realized for the first time throughout my whole being that all things are fulfilled in the Unborn, and I gradually came to know my former sins." He took firm hold of the vital point of his enlightenment, that "all things are fulfilled in the Unborn." He was then twenty-five years old.

After that Bankei went to meet various Zen priests and told them of his spiritual experiences. Yet he had not yet met one he could regard as his true master. Though he believed in what he had attained, he found no one to share his belief. Eventually he went to Nagasaki to study under a Chinese priest called Tao-che Ch'ao-yüan and received there the seal of enlightenment at the age of thirty in the third month of 1652, after sixteen years of strict training.

Alex Wayman, a professor of religion at Columbia University, is a world-renowned scholar of Buddhist philosophy and the author of a book called *Buddhist Insight*. He writes that Bankei, who can be considered to have been self-enlightened, attained such "Buddhist insight" as a result of his rigorous quest. One who is consciously absorbed in the clear state of mind where there is no speck of dust and no fragment of thought can penetrate deep into the minds of others, for "when no discriminative thoughts arise, we see into the mind's core."

THE SENSE OF FEAR

Most people, perhaps as many as 99.99 percent, have a sense of fear. It is almost impossible to find anyone among ordinary people who does not. Given that virtually everyone possesses a sense of fear, it must therefore be a natural human attribute. In April 1939 I became a student in the Law Department at Tōhoku Imperial University. The acceptance rate had been one in seventy-seven. At first I looked upon my professors as something like gods. Very soon, though, I was overcome by an indelible sense of distrust, for I knew they were unofficially and secretly upholding military violence. I say this because not one was willing to stake his position as a professor at an Imperial University to come out in public and denounce the unhappy chasm both the state and the people had fallen into. I realized at that time that they were all slaves to their fear.

After the end of the war I read Woodward's *Some Sayings of the Buddha,* which I knew to be a summary of the teachings contained in the *Āgama Sutras.* I realized then that the Buddha's abandonment of palace, wife, and child and his ascetic practice in the forest had been motivated by fear and a desire to become liberated from it. The Buddha almost died in the forest, so hard were the ascetic exercises he undertook as he sought a way to gain liberation from his fear. The book makes it extremely clear that his training was strict indeed. I wanted to find out whether the *Āgama Sutras* were really accurate when they presented the Buddha's confession of his fear and the strictness of his training.

It irritated me to think that with more than 2,500 years separating me from the Buddha there was no way to verify this. What was clear, though, was that the Buddha had liberated himself from fear by keeping at the forefront of his mind the need to seek the answer unremittingly himself.

I resolved the problem of fear at the age of twenty-three,

when I received authentication of enlightenment from Ueki Rōshi of Unganji Temple. Long after that, in 1963 at the age of forty-five, I became involved in what became known as the "Iizuka Incident." Four of my employees had been arrested and detained, and a young public prosecutor with the Utsunomiya District Court called Itō was heard to say loudly in a public bar after a few drinks that my own arrest was only a matter of time. I was called upon to conquer my fear repeatedly, with this threat hanging over me as a daily reality. You see, conquering fear completely once does not mean it does not come again; for fear has the property of rising constantly in the mind. It is a truly troublesome thing, but it is an extremely important issue in terms of the spiritual life.

It is essential first to inquire into the origins of the fear being experienced. Many people live their lives without experiencing it, or even trying to experience it, and they therefore never escape from its clutches. Some might think that this is inevitable, given that people as a whole are deluded and ignorant. Yet I think it is important for people to know that they infuse great human wisdom into liberation from the sense of fear.

The Buddha came to realize that fear is merely a mental appearance brought into being by our own mind. According to Woodward's translation, the Buddha was able to eliminate fear when he dwelt in "the Ultimate Self." The *Heart Sutra* says, "No hindrance, therefore no fear." The mind is originally without form or shape. If one completely remains in this state, then fear will not exist. If people do not attempt to watch their minds intently, however, or even to consider the value of doing so, they will tend not to keep the state of the mind formless or shapeless, and they will ultimately be left to tremble before fear as a result. This is the fundamental tragedy of the deluded and ignorant person.

MEDITATION TRAINING

I once read in Mircea Eliade's *Yoga: Immortality and Freedom,* which was originally written in French and translated into English by Willard R. Trask, the sentence, "The road to nirvana leads to the possession of miraculous powers" (p. 177). These supernatural, or miraculous, powers are, he says, one of the five classes of "super knowledges": (1) *siddhi* (miraculous powers); (2) the divine eye; (3) divine hearing; (4) knowledge of others' thoughts; and (5) recollection of previous existences (p. 178). This classification derives from the list in Vasubandhu's great commentary of the fourth century, the Abhidharmakovśavyākhyā. Here *siddhi* is defined in terms of supernatural powers such as flying through the sky and making the body invisible. The divine eye is the ability to foresee people's futures by such means as seeing into the afterworld. Divine hearing is the ability to hear all words and all sounds freely. Knowledge of others' thoughts is the ability to know other people's states of mind and what they are thinking. Recollection of previous existences means the ability to remember vividly what has happened in all one's past lives. Enlightenment leads to the attainment of these powers. As the author notes, however, these powers are equally at the disposal of the non-Buddhist *yogin.*

The Buddha forbade his disciples to pursue these powers, however, since if they became enthralled by the magical things of this world, they might well forget their original

THE WISDOM OF THE BUDDHA   111

goal of nirvana. Eliade bases his contention on passages considered to be the actual words of the Buddha quoted from the *Majjhima-nikāya,* the *Saṁyutta-nikāya,* and the *Aṅguttara-nikāya* of the Pali Canon. Yoga is a careful study, and a highly reliable one.

You do understand, do you not? Buddhist enlightenment is related to the attainment of the five supernatural powers, but their attainment is not, the Buddha concluded, in itself the realization of enlightenment. All the same, we cannot ignore the fact that supernatural powers are closely related to enlightenment. During the thirty-two years I spent studying under Ueki Rōshi I witnessed with my own eyes instances so clear as to be remarkable that convinced me that the Rōshi possessed the power of knowing the thoughts of others.

Furthermore, the goal of human perfection is the attainment of enlightenment, and the practice of meditation is essential to the path. Meditation may take many forms. We have seen that Vasubandhu spoke of four stages of meditation; he also stated that achievement of the five supernatural powers depends upon the accomplishment of these four stages. The first stage in the practice of meditation leads to a condition in which not a speck of dust remains in the mind. Having attained this, it is then important to discover how to go deeper and deeper into meditation. For many people, tiring of their quest, even the attainment of a mind with no speck of dust is no small thing. Most of them will realize the actuality of the thoughts and fancies that float like clouds through their minds, and they will find with puzzlement that training themselves, though not easy, is the greatest task in human life. There are quite a few people in Tibet known as "living Buddhas," and it is said that they know the birthplace and parents' names of living Buddhas about to be born. This is an amazing demonstration of the divine eye, whose acquisition without doubt results from the practice of meditation from childhood at the risk of life.

Conclusion: Making the Most of the Now

THE TRUE NATURE OF SELF-INTEREST

The problem of self-interest is an eternal question, one which has shadowed us since humankind first began to live in groups, and one which, I think, will be with us for as long as the human race survives. It is probably natural that people should put their own benefit first, if the self they comprehend is that which is merely an object of sensory knowledge. Ramsay MacDonald, the first Labor prime minister of Great Britain, drew a picture of the future in his book *Socialism, Critical and Constructive,* which of course reflected the views of his cabinet. The final chapter, "Motives to Work," discusses the question of what motives were necessary to make people work in a socialist society that did not espouse the profit principle. MacDonald addressed the question in his own inimitable way. First, he said, having superintendents from among the workers themselves oversee the work will in itself be sufficient motivation. Second, he noted, there is the ethical outlook of the worker himself, the awareness that if he does not do a good day's work, he will be letting down society as a whole. MacDonald's whole argument is based on the premise that if the basic conditions of social life change, people's hearts will change as well. I wonder.

The economist Maynard Keynes presented an opposing view. In *General Theory of Employment, Profit, and Money*, he said that, since self-interest is inherent to human beings, people in a society that does not allow the pursuit of profit will devote themselves to scheming to acquire power. With which of the two writers would you agree?

After human beings emerge from the womb and gradually begin to comprehend the existence of a world outside themselves, their awareness of their own ego grows and they learn to distinguish between themselves and the outer world. Because this idea of self is based on sensory perceptions, they seek out things that are comfortable and fulfilling to that self. This is generally considered to be perfectly reasonable, and most people exist within this mental framework, maturing, living, and finally dying within it. There are some, however, who are like the young Buddha, who in his youth perceived the suffering inherent in sickness, old age, and death and wished to escape from it and the fears it engendered. As a result of his investigation into the nature of these phenomena, he discovered the realm of the Tathāgata, the "Thus-gone One" who has attained enlightenment and escaped from the cycle of birth and death.

This is the result of taking one or two steps away from the

mental framework of ordinary life and from the habitual way of thinking, confronting the spiritual dimension head-on and cutting deep into it to seek the answers to one's questions. One who practices in this way realizes that self-interest is derived from a fatal misunderstanding of the most fundamental problem within his own being. It is the result of a great misunderstanding of oneself by oneself and a mental state of ignorance regarding the true self. People are astonished when they discover their real self. I was no different. The wonder of the realization that there is no "I," that "I" is nowhere to be found, reverberated through my whole body. What enables us to penetrate this truth is the koan in the seventh case recorded in the *Blue Cliff Record,* "One phrase of the Pre-Voice, ten thousand sages have not handed down." This is the question that asks what was your original face before your parents were born. It provided me with the means of cutting through the roots of self-interest.

THE IMPORTANCE OF FORGING SELF-CONTROL

Let us scrutinize the facts of our life objectively. The blood flowing through our veins and the cells that make up our body have been transmitted to us by ancestors without number. We ourselves were created by our parents, who in turn were born of theirs. The number of people of whom we are a direct descendant is mind-boggling. Counting back just a thousand or so years, to not long before Canute was telling the waves to retreat or the equivalent of around forty-one generations, our ancestors number well over three trillion. Counting back to the time of the reputed ancestor of the human race, *Pithecanthropus,* the number of ancestors swells to thousands of trillions. Our ancestors must have been of many types, including criminals, murderers, and thieves as well as good people. In biological terms we have indisputably inherited all of those factors in our makeup. This has determined the type of person we are now and given us the ability to go in any direction we choose.

The self we are now has been formed by all the various interactions between ourselves and others: the care we received when we were still in the womb; discipline at home; our school education; relationships with people in our neighborhood; and all the other virtually countless types of social interaction we have experienced. The direction we take and the way we are brought up are first decided by others; later, we ourselves take over the actions that serve to regulate our behavior. What we are today is the result of such self-control, as we have faced ourselves and decided how we should act or think, which course we should take, or how we should or should not behave. If this sense of self-control is weak, then inertia will in most cases pull us from one direction to another. I was like this, so I understand it from personal experience.

Among the writings prized in Rinzai Zen is the collection of koan called the *Gateless Gate* (Chinese *Wu-men-kuan;* Japanese *Mumonkan*). It contains forty-eight "cases," beginning with Chao-chou's "Mu" and ending with Kan-feng's "One road." In the twelfth case is a koan called "Jui-yen's master." I found the word "master" particularly interesting and asked Ueki Rōshi to write the word in large characters for me more than forty years ago, as I wanted to frame it and hang it in my home to provide a focus for self-admonition. Besides writing out the characters for me, he wrote beside them the following lines from the original text of the *Gateless Gate:*

Priest [Shih-]yen of Jui-yen [Temple] called to himself every day [upon waking], "Master!" and replied to himself, "Yes sir!" Then he would say, "Be wide awake!" and reply, "Yes sir!" At other times and on different days, "Do not be deceived by others!" "No sir!"

This koan urges Zen practitioners to know their true Self and to bring it with them.

I would like to comment on this from a different angle. Like Shih-yen's self calling the self, we should make it a point to call to ourselves in our daily round: "Be in the best of spirits today!" "Yes." "Live today according to the self of no-thought!" "Yes!" "Don't tell lies today!" "No!" To forge a mind such as this that enables us to control the self is of utmost importance in human life.

SEEING THE MOUNTAIN, NOT SEEING THE MOUNTAIN

More than twenty years ago I included in my *Fundamentals for Accountants* (Kaikeijin no genten) the words "Seeing the mountain, not seeing the mountain" as a vital component of the Zen experience. The topic came up again during a New Year's visit in 1991 by Mr. Miyamoto of TIMS and his wife, and I would like to relate it here.

Hōjō Tokimune (1251–1284), the de facto ruler of Japan in the mid-thirteenth century, practiced Zen seriously under the tutelage of Wu-hsüeh Tsu-yüan (1226–1286), a refugee from Mongol rule in China. Another of Wu-hsüeh's close disciples was the third son of the Emperor Go-Saga, Kōhō Kennichi (1241–1316), also known by his posthumous title

Bukkoku Kokushi, the founder of Unganji Temple, under whose fifty-eighth successor Ueki Rōshi I studied Zen for thirty-two years. There is a small hall on the hill behind Unganji called the Three Buddhas Hall. In the garden in front of the hall is a plaque with the verse Wu-hsüeh wrote when he knew death was approaching, following the custom of all Zen priests.

> Coming, nothing goes forward;
> Going, nothing retreats.
> A lion in every pore
> A lion roaring in every pore.

Though something or someone appears before him, he has no idea that "someone has come." Though he sees something or someone depart, he maintains no such concept as "I will see him off." Such a condition is like having lions roaring in every pore of the body.

This is an important issue for human life. René Descartes (1596–1650) said, "I think, therefore I am" *(Cogito ergo sum)*. He thought that "I" was something real, that it existed when thoughts appeared in the head. Therefore, he declared, there is no "I" when no thought exists (Descartes, *A Discourse on Method*, trans. John Veitch, Everyman's Library, 1949, p. 88). Descartes's mistake was that he was unable to realize that the Original Self is to be found when there is nothing in one's thoughts, when no thought exists in the mind.

The seventeenth century was a time in which great philosophers who were to exert an enormous influence over European civilization appeared throughout Europe, and it provided the bounds within which Descartes worked.

Descartes's "I" is no more than the "small I" of Zen Buddhism, the one-dimensional "I" created by the senses and existing only within the thoughts of the physical body. The great Japanese Zen master Shidō Bunan (1603–1676) wrote:

> Kill, kill,
> Kill the self,
> Kill it completely.
> When nothing is left,
> Become a teacher of others.

When one obliterates one's own consciousness, when not a speck of thought mars the surface of one's mind, the true Self, that is, the self which lives within the "great I," is revealed. Then one is worthy to become a teacher of others. In the *Āgama Sutras* we see how the Buddha, seeking the "Ultimate Self," came to the realization of the "objectless concentration of mind." This is the spiritual ideal of the Japanese, fostered in the Eastern way of thought, and the ideal form of Japanese mentality, which is not satisfied by the simple view of self held by Descartes and his followers. As internationalization grows increasingly strong, this is the principle of understanding the mind that the Japanese must export.

Such was the conversation I had with the Miyamotos during that New Year's four years ago.

ATTITUDES TOWARD ADVERSITY

"Face your deficiencies and acknowledge them; but do not let them master you. Let them teach you patience, sweetness, insight. . . . When we do the best we can, we never know what miracle is wrought in our life, or in the life of another." These are the words of Helen Keller (1880–1968), blind, deaf, and unable to speak. What fine words they are, and how strong the person who spoke them! Imagine how you would feel if you were blind, and then add to that not being able to hear or speak! Few human beings are ever as cruelly handicapped as this. From the point of view of those without handicaps, the suffering of such people seems unbearable.

A Japanese woman called Hisako Nakamura suffered from cataplectic gangrene at the age of three, and her limbs had to be amputated. Not one yen did she seek in government assistance in all her seventy-two years (she died in March 1968). As I read her biography, a copy of which I received from its author, Shōjirō Kurose, who attended a lecture of mine at the TKC Osaka Summer University, the tears streamed down my face many times. She was an enlightened person, who despite her hard fate could write, "My limbless body has been my teacher."

She met Helen Keller at a public meeting in Tokyo on April 17, 1937, which was also attended by the prime minister and other government ministers. Kurose describes the scene as follows: Iwahashi spoke in English in great detail about Hisako. This was transmitted to Helen by Thomson's signing. She clasped Hisako tightly and kissed her. She gently stroked Hisako's shoulders with both her hands and touched the short arms beneath her sleeves. When she touched Hisako's lower body, her face worked for a moment when Hisako understood she had artificial legs. Suddenly she embraced Hisako and kissed her for some time. Tears streamed from Helen's eyes. "She is much more unfortunate than I," the newspaper reported Helen as saying, "and a much greater person." Hisako was crying, too, and leaned against Helen's shoulder instinctively. Not one person in the crowd of more than two thousand could raise his or her face; for a moment, the auditorium was engulfed in silence, and then it was filled with sobbing. Helen returned to her seat, holding the doll she had received from Hisako and stroking it from head to toe, wiping her tears with her handkerchief (p. 228).

I cried many times as I transcribed this passage. The suffering borne by those women was not of their own making; it had been visited upon them. Nevertheless, they did not rail at fate, but faced their disabilities head-on. They lost neither their gratitude to the universe that sustained them nor their love toward their fellow human beings. The depth of their humanity and compassion is almost beyond words. Would I have such sympathy for others I if I were in their situation? Would I be able to live in gratitude with such a handicap without bemoaning my fate? I doubt it.

It is clear from the lives of Helen Keller and Hisako Nakamura that they faced their suffering directly, giving thanks for the fact that they were alive and bearing true love for others. They seem to say through their actions that to do otherwise would not have been in accordance with their true self. My own life would certainly be mean indeed if I could not help the disabled in any way possible. I salute you!

KILL, KILL, KILL THE SELF, KILL IT COMPLETELY. WHEN NOTHING IS LEFT, BECOME A TEACHER OF OTHERS

This is the verse of Shidō Bunan I mentioned briefly above. It tells us to obliterate all remnants of egotistical consciousness, for it is only then that we are worthy of becoming teachers of others. In *Fraternity*, the English novelist John Galsworthy asks, "What is love?" and answers, "Love is to forget oneself."

Obliterating the egotistical consciousness, that is, eliminating all sense of separation between the self and others and wiping the mind clean of any stain, is regarded in Western philosophy as well as in Buddhism as the highest form of the mind. Nevertheless, people who assume the self to be real and who base their actions on their own potential gain or loss are in the vast majority, while those who do not place themselves first in their actions tend, on the other hand, to be regarded as somewhat strange, as not living in the real world.

I am convinced that all people should come to grips with a problem such as that presented in the seventh case of the *Blue Cliff Record:* "One phrase of the Pre-Voice, ten thousand sages have not handed down." That means, "Say the word that is the self before your parents were born! Not one phrase of this have the sages handed down." If you think you are real, something that is forever unchanging, tell me what you looked like before your parents were born. Can you answer? You will realize that your "reality" is only a temporary form and that it originally has no permanence. It is important, too, to understand that phrases like "kill the self," or "kill the self completely" do not refer to making yourself a sacrifice and going along with the majority. Nor is there any objection implied here to asserting yourself. Note that I am in no way saying uncritical acceptance is important, and I do not think, either, that uncritical acceptance is a native characteristic of the Japanese. It is better that we take a firm grip on our own temporary existence, bring our breathing into the rhythm of the universe, and speak forth. Seeing the Japanese as exhibiting uncritical acceptance is a kind of misunderstanding. If it takes root, international society will continue to judge the Japanese mistakenly as people who are difficult to understand. As proof that the Japanese are not inherently uncritical, however, we have well over 500,000 literary works published between the eighth century and 1868. A glance at the recently published eight-volume *Catalogue of Japanese Writings* (which deals with works published during this time span) confirms the abundance of Japanese works and invites the question of whether any other country can rival that output. I showed the *Catalogue* to an American friend of mine, pointing out to him how each work was listed with its author and present location. He gave a whistle of surprise and marveled at the number. Given the number of books produced in premodern times by the efforts of their ancestors, I think the Japanese should have more confidence in their own intellectual caliber when meeting people from other countries and should make a point of telling the world of their vast cultural and historical inheritance, confident of its important place in the world.

BENEFITING BOTH SELF AND OTHERS

Society is flooded with advice. I find it strange that giving advice should have become such a business. I would like to ask, though, if those advisers are themselves successful. I know, for example, a fortune-teller who speaks of the mysteries of luck and good fortune to others, yet secretly bewails his own misfortune. His work is no more than a business, a means of making a living. There seems to be no proof of the effectiveness of fortune-telling in his case; he has been divorced three times. Why isn't he able to look into his own future and avoid his fate? Feeling sorry for him I used to think I should talk to him about it, but I never pursued it. When all is said and done, it is not anyone else's problem. There is a big difference between what people say and what they actually have the ability to do.

Imagine you were in charge of sales, in the widest meaning of the word. Would you question yourself closely if you were occupied only with the desire for a good sales record, which is comparable to strong-smelling bean paste that is not of the best quality? Would your customers notice that you were filled with a desire to post a good sales record? You would make little progress if they then decided you were only approaching them as part of your sales strategy. Strong-smelling bean paste is an inferior product. To sell it, you have to put your own ambition completely out of your mind. This is the essence of benefiting both the self and others. Do you then approach the customer thinking only of his or her own benefit, his or her own good? In most cases, your customers will be more experienced socially than you are. So it is important to know that they will instantly notice if you are inwardly eager to get good results. You consequently need to direct your full attention to the question of where true benefit to the customer lies. If you do not know what is necessary in terms of theory and psychology, you will be unable to accomplish business that truly benefits others. Study future trends from a variety of angles and create good customer relationships based on trust and reliability. This is not easy. It all goes back to how you confront yourself, and it depends on how much you truly believe in "benefiting both the self and others." Unless your actions stem from a strong philosophical conviction, your own life will never be one thing or another. In fact, most salaried workers lead second-rate lives.

I have referred already to Takeko Kujō, a very famous poet before the war. I still tend to sit up straight whenever I remember the words of her famous poem:

> Just look!
> Even the blossoms that are destined to fall tomorrow
> Are blooming now in their life's glory.

Here is the ideal of human life, the way that Zen expects it to be. Ueki Rōshi once said to me, "Iizuka, I live every day to the fullest!" Zen should not be just something cerebral. We must seek what Śākyamuni, the Buddha, called "objectless concentration of mind."

Human beings live less than a hundred years. When we look back on life we will find it extremely short. In the time given us, we should live every day to the fullest. Our life should not be motivated by an expectation of results, however, but by what Socrates called "holy action," the *Bhagavad Gita* "Krishna consciousness," and Kant "transcendental consciousness." These have been called the greatest way of living, the supreme form of the mind. They cost nothing in monetary terms. As long as we are alive in the world, let us spend our days in "holy action."

Appendix 1: The New Era of Auditing and the Accounting System of Japan, Part 1 (October 1990)

1. FROM BOOKKEEPING TO ACCOUNTING

On November 10, 1494, the text explaining the system of double-entry bookkeeping was unveiled to the world for the first time. The text is contained in Chapter X ("Tractatus Particularis de Computis et Scripturis") of the famous book on mathematics entitled *Summa de Aritmetica, Geometria Proportioni et Proportionalita* written by the Italian monk Lucas Pacioli (1445–1514). Although double-entry bookkeeping was practiced in various commercial republics of Italy in the Middle Ages, it was kept as a professional secret among the few who practiced record-keeping at the time.*

* Incidentally, the bookkeeping practices of wooden shoe merchants of Nürnberg during the Middle Ages is described in *Das Handlungsbuch der Holzschuher in*

Thus, Lucas Pacioli was the first person to publicize the principle of double-entry bookkeeping in a scientific publication. Moreover, fifty years before the publication of Pacioli's book, typography (the printing press) was invented by Johann Gutenberg, which greatly contributed to the dissemination of Pacioli's work.

However, during this period, the concept of the balance sheet was unknown, since annual settlement was not a custom at that time. The balance sheet appeared in the seventeenth century when France legislated it in its Ordonnance du Commerce in 1673. The balance sheet and financial statements were set as legal requirements under this code. This provision significantly affected the commercial codes of some other European nations during the eighteenth century, and the study of bookkeeping moved from Italy to France and Great Britain.

Matthieu de la Porte's *La Science des Negociants et Des Tenue de Livres*, published in 1712, is one of the most valuable works on bookkeeping in France. He experimented with the rational classification of accounts, stressed the fact that a business enterprise was a separate economic entity, distinct from its owner(s), and formulated the basis for the legal existence of business enterprises. Bertrand François Barreme follows de la Porte in the history of bookkeeping.

Nürnberg von 1304–1307, published in 1934, which was presented to me by my best friend, Dr. Heinz Sebiger, on November 25, 1984, at a dinner following the ceremony in celebration of the completion of DATEV III. This work is a ledger based on the principle of double-entry and the articles of *Vollstaendige Eintragung in das Handlungsbuch* (complete entry into the commercial book), which makes one assume that the concept of evidential competency *(Beweiskraft)* of the books of account was near to its establishment.

He classified the accounts into general accounts and special accounts in his *Traité des Parties Doubles,* published in 1721. This classification system was paramount in French bookkeeping until the late nineteenth century.

As for eighteenth century works on bookkeeping in Great Britain, one should note *The Complete English Tradesman,* published in 1725 by Daniel Defoe (1660–1731), the famous author of *Robinson Crusoe;* John Mair's *Bookkeeping Methodized,* published in 1741, which was appraised as the standard of the period; and *Jones English System of Bookkeeping by Single or Double Entry,* published in 1796 by the accountant Edward Thomas Jones of Bristol. However, the English system of bookkeeping was considered by some as merely an expanded form of single-entry bookkeeping. Jones's work was criticized by the economist James Mill (1773–1836) in *An Examination of Jones English System of Bookkeeping,* where he pointed out that there was no way to check embezzlement under the English system. Mill's analysis demonstrated that double-entry bookkeeping superseded any other bookkeeping method.

In the nineteenth century, bookkeeping theory was mainly concerned with balance accounts. *Buchhaltungssystem und Buchhaltungsforme,* published in 1887 by Friedrich Huegli (1833–1902), an accounting official in Bern, Switzerland, and *Buchhaltung und Bilanz,* published in 1914 by the business economist Johann Friedrich Schaer (1846–1925), had established the Materialistische Zweikontenreihentheorie (Materialistic Theory of Two Accounts), which greatly influenced Japan and the United States. In the intellectual history of bookkeeping, the development of the concept of "controlling account" in the nineteenth century had an impact equivalent to that the Industrial Revolution had on economic history.

Dr. Kiyoshi Kurosawa, a Japanese Professor of accounting, pointed out in one of his famous books, *Accounting* (1933), that the beacon of distinction between the traditional and modern methods of bookkeeping must be based on the idea of controlling account (also referred to as "control account"). Thus, one can estimate the establishment of accounting between the end of the nineteenth century to the beginning of the twentieth. In particular, one must credit the establishment of accounting as a science to the publication of Eugen Schmalenbach's (1873–1955) *Dynamische Bilanz* in 1919 and Heinrich Nicklisch's (1876–1946) *Wirtschaftliche Betriebslehre* in 1922. The Institute of Chartered Accountants in England and Wales was established in 1880. Across the Atlantic, the New York State Society of Certified Public Accountants was established in 1897, following the enactment of the Certified Public Accountant Law of New York State in 1896. Note that these professional organizations were formed almost simultaneously with the establishment of the science of accounting.

2. THE BEGINNING AND THE NEW ERA OF AUDITING

In June of 1853 Commodore Matthew Perry (1794–1858) entered Japan. He presented the credentials from President Millard Fillmore to the Shoganate, and in March of the following year the U.S.-Japan Treaty was concluded. This preceded peace treaties that Japan concluded with other countries such as Great Britain, Russia, and Holland. Thus, the U.S.-Japan Treaty played an important role in introducing Japan to the Western world. Ninety-one years after the signing of the U.S.-Japan Treaty, Japan was defeated in World War II and passed into American occupation under General Headquarters (GHQ). Despite the loss, this was a very happy experience for Japan and its people. Since the reason is quite evident, I believe that it need not be explained in detail here. Under the occupation Japan learned much from the United States and was able to eventually become one of the leading economic nations of the world.

In 1948, the Certified Public Accounting Law was endowed to the Japanese under the supervision of GHQ. Gradually, we started auditing based on the principles learned from the United States. The professors of accounting lecturing in Japanese universities, especially those who were lecturing on auditing theory, studied works such as Montgomery's *Auditing, Auditing Principles and Procedures* by Arthur W. Holmes, C.P.A., *Auditing Standards and Procedures* by Homes and Burns, and *The Philosophy of Auditing* by Robert K. Mautz and Hussein A. Sharaf. These were indeed valuable references to teach Japanese students.

Apart from the aforementioned books, I have the following books at my disposal:

1. AICPA, *Professional Standards, U.S. Auditing Standards*
2. AICPA, *Audit and Accounting Manual* (non-authoritative technical practice guide)
3. Jack C. Robertson, *Auditing,* 6th edition
4. Donald H. Taylor and G. William Glezen, *Auditing: Integrated Concepts and Procedures,* 4th edition

5. Dan M. Guy, C. Wayne Alderman, and Aland J. Winters, *Auditing,* 2nd edition
6. Meigs, Whittington, Pany, and Meigs, *Principles of Auditing,* 9th edition
7. Walter G. Kell, William C. Boynton, and Richard E. Ziegler, *Modern Auditing,* 4th edition
8. D. R. Carmichael and John J. Willingham, *Auditing Concepts and Method: A Guide to Current Auditing Theory and Practice,* 5th edition
9. D. R. Carmichael and John J. Willingham, *Perspectives in Auditing,* 4th edition
10. Martin A. Miller and Larry P. Bailey, *Comprehensive GAAS Guide 1990*
11. The Institute of Chartered Accountants in England and Wales, *Auditing and Reporting 1989/90.*

Each of the above is superior on its own and all are grand works. However, I am not satisfied with them in the intellectual sense. The reason is this: Auditing is really the action of human beings. The actions of human beings are formed through the interrelationships of the conditions between the subject of human beings and the object of their cognition. No matter how logically well prepared one is regarding the objects of cognition, as long as the conditions of the subject of human beings have not matured ordinary negligence or gross negligence shall be unavoidable. Accordingly, the "Wave of Litigation" becomes apparent. I think this is the atmosphere at present in the United States.

The German philosopher Edmund Husserl (1859–1938) commented in his book *Ideen zu einer reinen Phaenomenologie und Phaenomenologischen Philosophie* (Ideas Pertaining to Pure Phenomenology and to a Phenomenological Philosophy), published in 1913, that "we find a remarkable polarity in every act: on the one side, the ego-pole as 'Noesis' and to the object pole as 'Noema'." The present state of auditing seems to be only pursuing the preciseness of *Noema*. However, I believe that to prepare for *Noesis*, the training in what Immanuel Kant called "transzendentales Bewusstsein" (transcendental consciousness) is the best way to achieve the utmost form of auditing. And this is very different from the "mysticism" that Professors Mautz and Sharaf referred to in their book.

The concept of mysticism or "a priori judgment" that Professors Mautz and Sharaf referred to will be one of the important clues to lead us to the solution. The development of "an intuitive ability," which is mentioned in the eighth edition of Montgomery's *Auditing,* shall also provide us with a very important key to it. Therefore, there certainly exists the best attainable means to develop the new era of auditing with the transcendental consciousness of our daily lives. Herein lies the point that auditing professionals in the United States may someday discover they need to learn from the Orient; that is, the philosophy of transcendental consciousness found in the *Veda Philosophy,* a document written some five thousand years ago in India. In it one can find the teachings of the principles of how the best condition of human consciousness should be.

3. THE ACCOUNTING SYSTEM OF JAPAN

Whenever I talk about the accounting system of Japan, I cannot help but be embarrassed. For example, if you examine the 1990 edition of *Kaikei Zensho* (Compendium on accounting), under "Principles of Corporate Accounting," you will find just four pages. Even if you add the "Standards of Cost Accounting," it will still be only twenty pages. Regrettably, if you consider "The Principles of Consolidated Financial Statements," "The Accounting Standards for Foreign Currency Transactions," "The Accounting Standards for Public Interest Corporations," and "The Accounting Standards for School Incorporation" as well, it will still total just fifty-nine pages of authoritative discussion. By contrast, in the 1990 edition of *Comprehensive GAAS Guide,* there are 1,108 pages of discussion relating to accounting standards in the United States of America. Clearly one can see a gap between the accounting system of Japan and that of the United States.

Moreover, to my lament, this gap does not exist only between Japan and the United States, but between Japan and the United Kingdom as well. In the 1989/1990 edition of *Accounting Standards* published by the Institute of Chartered Accountants in England and Wales, you will find 678 pages relating to the relevant standards. However, because the print size in the English publication is smaller than the print size in the American publication, I believe that there is not much difference in the amount of material.

The gap exists in terms of auditing standards as well. Under "Auditing Standards," "Working Rules of Auditing Procedures of Field Work," "Working Rules of Audit Procedures in Reporting Standards," and "Standard of Interim Audit of Financial Statements" one finds thirteen pages in the 1990 *Kaikei Zensho.* By contrast, in the 1990 *Comprehensive GAAS Guide,* one finds 1,368 pages and in the 1989/

90 *Auditing and Reporting,* one finds 1,074 pages. Clearly there is a drastic gap between Japan and these two countries. What could be the causes of such a drastic gap? Let me give you three explanations. These views are solely my own opinion on the subject.

First of all, the Japanese Principles of Accounting and other related standards are not based on any kind of legality. The Business Deliberation Council established in 1952 by an ordinance of the Japanese Ministry of Finance is not, and has never been, as powerful organ as the Securities and Exchange Commission (SEC), which was established under the U.S. Securities Exchange Act of 1934, Section 4. The SEC has the right to enact rules and regulations under Articles 11, 17, and 23. Thus, those who intentionally violate SEC rules or regulations could be subjected to monetary fine or imprisonment. When such a violation is committed by an exchange dealer, the penalty could be up to $500,000. Apart from this, the SEC has the right of "investigations, injunctions and prosecutions of offenses" (Section 21) against those who are suspected of violating the rules and regulations. Thus, one can easily see that the distribution of powers to national agents is quite different in Japan as compared to the United States.

The second reason, in my opinion, is the confrontation between the Japanese Ministries of Finance and Justice, which originated from a discord between the Financial Accounting Deliberation Council and the Legislative Council. Furthermore, this situation can be traced back to the confrontation between the Japanese scholars of accounting who were members of the Financial Accounting Deliberation Council and the Japanese scholars of law who were members

of the Legislation Council. It is apparent to me that the fe
of this opposition can be found in more that thirty artic
within the *Kaikei Zensho* and confirmed by the various stat
ments released by the Financial Accounting Deliberatioi
Council. This opposition and the continued discord has per-
sisted for more than thirty years and has been exposed to the
rest of the world by the release of official statements. This is
indeed an unheard of disgrace, and I believe that you can all
imagine, by now, how incompetent the Japanese politicians
are who have left this matter unresolved. It is a problem
resulting from the lack of courage and intelligence.

The third reason can be found in the Japanese Commercial
Code, Article 12, Clause 2, which states, "In interpreting the
provisions concerning the preparation of the account books,
reasonable accounting practice shall be taken into consideration." This statement is based on the theory espoused by
Professor Kotaro Tanaka in *The Logic of the Balance Sheet
Law* published in 1944. Professor Tanaka was a renowned
scholar, Dean of the Law Department of the University of
Tokyo, Minister of Education, and the President of the Japanese Supreme Court. Professor Tanaka stated that in matters
relating to the reconciliation of commercial bookkeeping one
must follow "the rules and regulations of regular bookkeeping" under German law. However, the meaning of "rules
and regulations of regular bookkeeping" is not stated in
Professor Tanaka's theory. In one sense it means that exclud-
ing the case for establishing a certain rule for individual
points of importance, the law maker must acknowledge the
existence of principal regulations generally practiced among
the corporations, and that a blank rule shall be established
whose details are delegated to actual practices. In this case,

it means that the content of the actual practice that has been delegated must be of a legal nature. This is the meaning that prevails in Japan. But this is not the meaning according to German law, nor is it in American or English laws.

Surprisingly, Japanese scholars of commercial law never doubted Professor Tanaka's theory and obeyed it unanimously. This is based on the fact that Professor Tanaka was the highest authority in Japanese jurisprudence at the time. According to Professor Tanaka's theory, there is no need to set factual rulings for necessary "matters that are considered as fair accounting practices." Professor Tanaka's theory is directly reflected in Japan's Corporation Tax law (Article 22, Clause 4) and the Regulation of Financial Statements (Article 1). The concept of "Fair accounting practices" stated in Japan's Commercial Code (Article 32, Clause 2), the concept of "Generally Accepted Accounting Principles" stated in the Corporation Tax Law (Article 22, Clause 4), and the concept of "Generally Accepted Corporation Accounting Standards" stated in the Regulations for Financial Statements (Article 1) all share Professor Tanaka's theory, although there may be some difference in the wording.

4. CONCLUDING REMARKS

Essentially, Japanese accounting standards and auditing standards are accepted as is, while this is not the case in most advanced countries like the United States, United Kingdom and Germany. Thus, there is a grave defect regarding the number of norms in the Japanese accounting system as compared to these countries. Although this defect or gap is compensated by the "Chancellor's Circular of the National Tax

Administration Agency," this is referred to as an assertion, a compilation of the customary interpretations of standards by the high officials of the Ministry of Finance. Most people view this as de facto legislation by the officials of the Ministry of Finance. Moreover, this is a deficiency when compared to the United States, where the rulings for the administration of tax matters are formed based on the official explanations of tax laws.

For more than ten years I have been appealing for the necessity to correct this grave defect regarding the rules and regulations governing accounting in Japan. The Ministry of Finance has finally come to an understanding of the defect and has sanctioned the establishment of the Foundation of Corporate Financial System Research Association on July 2, 1990.

Appendix 2: The New Era of Auditing and the Accounting System in Japan, Part 2

In my lecture on October 10, 1990, at the Arthur K. Solomon auditorium of New York University, I said:

No matter how one is logically well prepared regarding the objectives of cognition, for as long as the conditions of the subject side of human beings may not become matured, "Ordinary Negligence" or "Gross Negligence" shall be unavoidable. Accordingly, "the Wave of Litigation" becomes so common. And I think this is the actual atmosphere at present of the auditing practice in the United States.

Furthermore, I also quoted the following words: "We find a remarkable polarity in every human act: on the one side, the Ego-pole; on the other, the object as the counter-pole." This passage was taken from the book *Ideen zu einer reinen Phä-*

nomenologie und phänomenologischen Philosophie (Ideas pertaining to a pure phenomenology and to a phenomenological philosophy, 1913), written by Edmund Husserl (1859–1938). Husserl used Greek terminology, namely, *Noesis* and *Noema,* in referring to the ego-pole and the counterpole, respectively.

As far as I can understand, I believe the United States standards for accounting and for auditing, as *Noema,* are obviously the most advanced ones in the world in terms of their accuracy, comprehensiveness, and intellectual level. Accordingly, I observe that Americans appreciate from the bottom of their hearts truthfulness, fairness, and transparency even in the field of accounting. The pursuit of these values has made them achieve their excellent circumstances. At the same time, I have two concerns. First, as far as American CPAs try to secure truthfulness, fairness, and transparency for the society, accounting and auditing standards need a police power so that they can be enforced. However, as accounting and/or auditing standards approach the limit of accuracy, they may bring an unbearable burden to the enterprises or to professional accountants. When and how the United States will define certain border lines in this field is the question.

The second concern regards audit textbooks at universities in the United States. While I admit that the objectivity and accuracy of the theory in these books is quite superior, there is one fundamental thing lacking: the theory of human behavior. For auditing, in its bare essence, is no more than a human activity. If we therefore listen to what Husserl said about human behavior as *Noesis,* it becomes clear that auditors and accountants need to train themselves to find the way

to develop their intuitive power or transcendental consciousness. The subject of transcendental consciousness is not only
a matter of simple care, merely looking at the surface as if
heeding a knock on the door, but concerns finding the way
and to what extent one can establish the concrete way to
discover clearly the subject side of one's mind. Of course I
cannot see any indications of awareness of this important
principle in Japanese universities, which are remarkably far
behind American universities regarding accounting and
auditing due to their tendency simply to learn from the
United States. As long as transcendental consciousness remains so weak, the Wave of Litigation against professional
accountants will become more serious day by day. Therefore
I really pray that American professional accountants or
CPAs may realize the necessity of Zen training or self-dis-
covering. This principle of polishing the transcendental consciousness originated from India, then transferred to China,
and finally came to Japan. It has remained only in Japan up
to now.

I visited Germany last June, and fortunately I had the
opportunity to have a discussion with my best friend, Dr.
Heinz Sebiger, President of DATEV, the largest information
and data processing organization for professional accountants in Germany, and Dr. Wilfreid Dann, chairman of the
German Institute of Tax Laws and of the German Federation
of the Chambers of Tax Consultants. On that occasion Dr.
Dann and I concluded that German CPAs have not suffered
from the Wave of Litigation as the American CPAs have
because of two provisions of the Wirtschaftsprüferordnung,
the German CPA Law. One of them regards *Verjährung*
(prescription) (prescribed in SS 51,70). Prescription pertains

to the exemption from liabilities for damages after three or five years, as the case may be. The other one pertains to the legal requirement of the law called Kreditwesen-Gesetz (Banking Law) for the auditee to submit a *Vollständigkeits-erklärung* (declaration of completeness). These two legal stipulations provide the breaks for litigation. I would be happy if these two points could serve as a reference to American CPAs.

I also mentioned in my lecture last October that with regard to accounting principles there is a drastic gap between Japan and the United States, with Japan being far behind. Moreover, this drastic gap does not exist only between Japan and the United States but also between Japan and the United Kingdom. Similarly, as I also mentioned last year, there is a drastic gap between Japan and these countries regarding the number of rules in the standards of auditing. According to my observation there are three main causes that resulted in such drastic structural gaps between Japan and the two countries.

First, accounting arinciples in Japan do not have legal authority. The Business Accounting Deliberation Council in Japan, which was established in 1952 by "The Act of Establishing the Ministry of Finance," failed to win in giving legal status, or meaning and dignity, to the accounting principles in Japan. A German legal philosopher and scholar of Roman Law, Dr. Rudolph von Jhering (1818–1892) said in one of his famous works, *Der Kampf ums Recht* (The Fight for the Right): "Das Ziel des Rechts ist der Friede, das Mittel dazu ist der Kampf" ("the purpose of the law is the peace, the means of realizing it is the fight"). However, the scholars who composed the Business Accounting Deliberation Council of Japan did not fight for accounting principles in Japan to have meaning or dignity as legal status, as Dr. Jhering defined it.

Let me show you how weak the Business Accounting Deliberation Council of Japan is by looking at the case of the United Kingdom. The United Kingdom passed a law known as the 1948 Companies Act, wherein Article 149 established the principle of "a true and fair view." When the time came to prepare the EC Directive for companies' accounts, the United Kingdom engaged in big theoretical argument for the adoption of this principle and the terminology of "a true and fair view" itself in the Fourth Directive of the EC. After ten years of persuasion, it finally succeeded in overriding committee members of the EC. In Japan, on the other hand, despite the fact known worldwide that the EC Directive contains six provisions of said accounting principle, the scholars who shaped the Business Accounting Deliberation Council did not make any effort to accomplish the same. I think any person connected with the accounting system in the world can decide how to evaluate this matter.

The second reason for the drastic gap, which is abnormal, I understand, is the conflict between the Ministry of Finance and the Ministry of Justice in Japan. I would say that this situation has resulted from the conflicts between the legal scholars who shaped the Legislative Deliberation Council of the Ministry of Justice, on the one hand, and the accounting scholars who shaped the Business Accounting Deliberation Council, on the other hand. I cannot but say that this is due to a little bit of exaggerated pride in scholars of law, on one hand, and a little bit too much of an inferiority complex in scholars of accounting, on the other. Too much pride and too much inferiority complex have been closely interwoven, so to speak.

This conflict between legal scholars and accounting scholars can be easily grasped by looking at a similar incident in Germany. Dr. Eugen Schmalenbach (1873–1955), a world-famous accounting scholar, particularly during the period of 1919 and thereafter in Germany, became furious when he issued the *Dynamische Bilanz* (Dynamic Balance Sheet) because no legal scholar accepted his work. This was despite the fact that his work was regarded as one of the world's greatest accounting books. Among the legal scholars who did not accept his work was Dr. Enno Becker (1869–1940), a German justice who originated single-handedly the Reichsabgabenordnung (National Tax Procedure Act) in Germany. I can also disclose the fact that a certain Japanese deputy director general of the Ministry of Justice, who was in charge of the Amendment to the Commercial Code, did not adopt in the amended Commercial Code of June 1990, the principle of "a true and fair view." As mentioned, this was adopted in the Fourth EC Directive. This officer refused despite my repeated appeal and advice to consider my suggestion for the adoption of this principle in the amended Code. The concerned Deputy Director General firmly stood his ground, saying that "EC people do not understand what the law is." You can see from such a statement the reason the principle was not finally adopted in the amended Code.

The third reason for this drastic gap is due to the provisions of the second clause of Article 32 of the Japanese Commercial Code, which reads: "For the purpose of interpretation of the rule regarding preparation of books of accounts, fair accounting customs should be deeply considered." This provision was adopted straight from the logic described in page 36 of the *Logic of Balance Sheet Law,* written by Dr. Kotaro Tanaka, then dean of the Department of Law at the University of Tokyo, in 1944. This logic, in brief, shows that the German Commercial Code is the mother law of the Japanese Commercial Code, although it is not clear what is shown in the Grundsätze ordnungsmässiger Buchführung (Principles of Regular Bookkeeping), Article 38 (the present Article 238) of the German Commercial Code.

In short, legislators adopted Dr. Tanaka's theory that

there must be practical principles which are generally being implemented among companies. Accordingly, the law should merely establish "blank provisions" and that detailed matters should be left to practical customs except for some important matters, and, only in those cases where details of the laws will be established. In other words, practices are thought to bear the character of the law.

Japanese accounting scholars and legal scholars unanimously believed in this "blank assignment theory." In this point there is a remarkable difference between Euro-American universities and Japanese universities. In Japan, particularly for the study of accounting and law, which are both not experimental but cultural sciences, nobody would try to oppose the opinion of a topmost leader and authority. Anybody who would oppose the opinion of such a person would have his life as a scholar substantially erased. In other words, he would not survive in society. I am ashamed to say it here, but it is a fact that many professors at Japanese universities have confessed this to me directly. It is a very terrible matter, but it is true.

On the contrary, in American and European universities, while disciples naturally appreciate their teachers, in the pursuit of scientific truth they never hesitate to say what they believe to their teachers. Dr. Gustav Radbruch (1878–1949) declared in his book *Rechtsphilosophie* (Legal Philosophy) (Achte Auflage S. 149), "Zur Personlichkeit wird man durch selbstvergessene Sachlichkeit" ("through the objectivity of forgetfulness of self, a man becomes true personality"). Dr. Radbruch was a professor of many regional German universities on legal philosophy. He was also the teacher of Dr. Kotaro Tanaka. I take this concept of Dr. Radbruch as the respectable, pure proposition of a scholar. In Zen Buddhist society in Japan there is an old saying: "never concede to your Zen master in case you are probing the ultimate self." In the world of Husserl's "Noesis" or Kant's "transcendental consciousness" such a calculating consciousness in the secular society does not exist even as a particle of dust floating in the air. Such a calculating consciousness is impure and incompatible with the situation of the person searching for the scientific truth.

The Conference of National, Regional and International Standard Setting Bodies met in Brussels, June 16–18, 1991, primarily to discuss and exchange opinions on the following three major points:

1. The necessity and object of conceptual framework as basis for financial report.
2. Usefulness of conceptual framework.
3. Possibility of cooperation among concerned standard setting bodies to proceed towards internationalization of accounting standards.

Professor A., chairman of the Business Accounting Deliberation Council of the Ministry of Finance, and Professor S., a member of this council, attended the conference as the representatives from Japan. The full text of the statement of the two professors (original in English) was issued in the September edition of *Accounting,* the bulletin of The Japan Society of Accounting, published by Moriyama Shoten in Tokyo. The title of their report was "Legal and Conceptual Framework of Accounting in Japan." I cannot avoid pointing out two defects in their report from my personal viewpoint, although it is a pity for me to criticize them here. However, I must make these defects clear since they are related to accounting systems in Japan. The first defect is the concluding comment:

Even though Business Accounting Deliberation Council attempts to set accounting standards under which, for example, the current market price is proposed as a valuation basis for marketable securities, or the mark-to-mark rule is proposed for futures transactions, it is impossible or quite difficult to finalize such standards.

This comment absolutely means that with respect to the amendment of the present laws, the members of the council have been giving up the fight from the start, contrary to what Dr. Rudolf von Jhering advised in his book. I am convinced that the field of accounting systems cannot evolve without paying homage to the work of other scholars.

The second defect is in the following comment:

As for the Corporate Income Tax Law, its 1947 amendments made it clear that corporate income tax should be computed based upon the income determined under the computation rules of the Commercial Law.

As I mentioned before, the Rules of Account in the Commercial Code are not sufficient to properly define how income tax calculation is now being performed, based on internal circulars being issued by the Director General of the National Tax Agency, which have grown in volume to a large number. The fact that accounting principles in Japan have no legal status and that they depend on the internal circulars of the Director General of the National Tax Agency, which has no legal authority on accounting matters, seriously threatens to impair and undermine the independence of the accounting profession in Japan. For the purpose of assuring the transparency, accuracy, and fairness of accounting systems as a basis for the preparation of financial statements in Japan, I strongly call for abolishing the tremendous volume of internal circulars of the National Tax Agency. Instead, make them all Enforcement Regulations based on Article 65 of Corporation Tax Law, by giving them legal authority. I strongly suggest that this would simply be following the decision of Chancellor Konrad Adenauer (1876–1967) of Germany in 1949, when the Grundgesetz (Constitution) (Clause 3, Article 20) was promulgated and all tax law circulars were abolished in Germany. I am quite sure that accounting systems in Japan can be improved by moving toward international standards regarding the two points I have mentioned above. Other matters shall be considered in the next lecture.

Appendix 3: The New Era of Auditing and the Accounting System in Japan, Part 3

A. THE NEW ERA OF AUDITING

1. Introduction

In my lecture on October 10, 1990 at the Arthur K. Salomon Auditorium at the Leonard N. Stern Business School of New York University, I made the following statement:

Auditing is really the action of human beings themselves. Actions of human beings are formed through the interrelationships of the conditions between the subject of human beings and the object of their cognition. No matter how one is logically well prepared regarding objectives of cognition, for as long as the conditions of the subject of human beings may not become matured, "Ordinary Negligence" or "Gross Negligence" shall be unavoidable. Accordingly, "the Wave of Litigation" becomes so common. And I think this is the actual atmosphere at present of the auditing practice in the United States.

Furthermore, I also quoted the following words: "We find a remarkable polarity in every act: on the one side, the Ego-pole; on the other, the object as counter-pole." This passage was taken from Husserl's *Ideas Pertaining to a Pure Phenomenology and to a Phenomonological Philosophy* (1913). Husserl called this Ego-pole *Noesis.* It is exactly what Immanuel Kant had called "transcendental consciousness" in his work. Husserl, too, frequently uses the term "transcendental consciousness" in his book. At issue is the acquisition of the idea of pure transcendental consciousness and how to enter the transcendental realm. I will focus my talk now on these two points.

2. The Issue of Acquiring the Idea of Transcendental Consciousness

The first issue concerns acquiring the idea of transcendental consciousness. The acquisition of ideas means the understanding of ideas. The cognition of ideas differs from the acquisition of ideas. In this case, words can be used interchangeably with ideas. But cognition, in the sense of a meeting of ideas and words, is something we experience on innumerable occasions. After going through countless experiences, by associating first with our parents, then with our brothers and sisters, teachers, schoolmates, neighbors, and people in the society, we encounter and recognize ideas and words. The cognition of ideas and words, however, is not necessarily identical to the understanding of ideas and words. Occasionally, we use ideas and words without knowing their real meaning. The same can be said about transcendental consciousness. We sometimes use ideas and words such as "transcendental consciousness" without knowing their real meaning.

Transcendental consciousness is consciousness that has not reached the level of experience: it is very far from concrete consciousness. Thus, the question arises whether consciousness without specific substance can be called consciousness. In *Discourse on Method,* Descartes said "Cogito ergo sum" ("I think therefore I am"). According to Descartes, one finds himself in his thoughts. Thus, the converse holds: One does not find himself where his thoughts do not exist. This expression implies that transcendental consciousness without substance is no longer consciousness. This means that we human beings have consciousness that is not consciousness in essence. One individual who thoroughly inquired into this question was the Buddha of India. I would now like to refer to *Some Sayings of the Buddha, According to the Pali Canon,* translated by F. L. Woodward and published by Oxford University Press in 1925. This is an abridged translation of the *Nikāyas,* the early Buddhist scriptures. According to this translation, Buddha left the palace at age twenty-nine and lived in the jungles. After six years of training, Buddha attained spiritual enlightenment (or nirvana) and thereafter traveled throughout India. Buddha preached for forty-five years and died at the age of ninety. His teachings are called Buddhism. Of these teachings, Mahayanist Buddhism was introduced into China and reached Japan via Korea. Since the official chronicles of Japan indicated that Mahayanist Buddhism reached Japan thirteen years after the enthronement of the Kinmei Emperor, this dates back about 1440 years. Nirvana is interpreted by Westerners as a state of nothingness, extinction of consciousness, or annihilation of consciousness. Western writers seem to understand nirvana as a complete vacuum. But the truth is the complete opposite of that. The actions and interests of those who attain nirvana are completely detached from all images and sound. But internally, the mind is "in a condition of most intense activity." Since the person is himself to the fullest stretch of his capacity, he is infinitely more himself. In this sense, it must be said that the idea of nirvana in Buddhism is on a higher level than the idea of transcendental consciousness explained by Husserl and Kant.

Let me repeat what I said at the outset:

Auditing is really the action of human beings themselves. Actions of human beings are formed through the interrelationships of the conditions between the subject of human beings and the object of their cognition. No matter how one is logically well prepared regarding objectives of cognition, for as long as the conditions of the subject side of human beings may not become matured, "Ordinary Negligence" or "Gross Negligence" shall be unavoidable. Accordingly, "the Wave of Litigation" becomes so common. And I think this is the actual atmosphere at present of the auditing practice in the United States.

In other words, the maturity of human subjective conditions has become an indispensable condition for the performance of effective auditing. This is not only a prerequisite for auditing. These conditions of the mind must be maintained during the act of auditing as well. In the *Nikāyas,* Buddha called these conditions of the mind "Objectless Concentration of Mind." This Objectless Concentration of Mind is an idea that is very close to, but differs slightly from, Kant's and Husserl's transcendental consciousness. Although this Objectless Concentration of Mind is in the same transcendental realm, it is a dynamic consciousness.

As stated previously, Mahayanist Buddhism emerged in ancient India and reached Japan via China and Korea. In India, China, and Korea, Mahayanist Buddhism has already become almost extinct. The arrival of Mahayanist Buddhism was a major cultural development for Japan more than a thousand years ago, but it has gained a firm foothold, in tune with the national characteristics of the Japanese people. It has endured more than a thousand winters and has become a culture indigenous to Japan. I firmly believe that the Objectless Concentration of Mind taught by the Buddha must be treated as the absolute foundation of the world's current auditing practices. This is the reason why I entitled my talk "The New Era of Auditing."

3. The Issue of How to Enter the Transcendental Realm

Before people think about how to enter the transcendental realm, they must realize that they have already entered the transcendental realm. Because of this, there is a possibility that the way in which this issue is posed will lead people to misunderstand the notion. About three hundred years ago, there lived a Zen priest by the name of Hakuin Ekaku (1685–1768). He was a distinguished Zen priest, deemed as a restorer of the Rinzaishu of Buddhism. Hakuin wrote a book called *Japanese Manifest of Zen*. In this book, he mentions "crying out in thirst while in the water." In this passage Hakuin wonders why the person in the water is complaining about thirst. Perhaps it is normal for us philistines to fail to become aware of transcendental consciousness because it is located too close to us. An interesting episode is still recounted in the headquarters of the Myoshin-ji sect. One day when Hakuin was preaching in the Ryotaku-ji temple a carpenter named Heishiro from Anbara Village appeared and listened to Hakuin's sermon behind the shoji. After Hakuin finished preaching Heishiro went into the bathroom of the temple and sat in Zen meditation for three days. It is said that he finally attained nirvana. This episode illustrates that it is not difficult at all to reach nirvana. Anyone can experience a state of Objectless Concentration of Mind through a comparatively short period of practice. I took seven years to attain this condition because I was slow in discovering that I was already in a state of constant transcendental consciousness and because I was hindered by ideas and wild fancies. The most difficult thing was realizing that I was constantly in a state of transcendental consciousness. In everyday life one is in a state of objectless consciousness for a much longer period of time than one is in a state of object consciousness. To discover this, one usually needs to practice meditation. Besides meditation, it is believed that the close examination of the behavior of one's mind is also essential. It is said that a mental condition that is one with the universe prevails during objectless concentration of mind. In Japan, it is believed that this condition is attained through Zen. But esoteric Buddhism places particular emphasis on this point.

B. ACCOUNTING SYSTEM IN JAPAN

1. Reform of the Auditing System in japan

On December 26, 1991, Japan undertook efforts to reform its auditing system in the form of an announcement by the Business Accounting Deliberation Council of the Ministry of Finance. These reforms called for revising the audit standards and the working rules of audit procedures of field work and reporting that form the foundation of functions performed by certified public accountants.

The revisions were made multilaterally. I think several items in particular stood out. First, under the name of "purification," among the rules for performing an audit before revision, the full text of "II. Ordinary Auditing Procedures" was deleted. In place of that, the Japanese Institute of Certified Public Accountants was positioned as the body responsible for establishing the standards that constitute the specific foundation of auditing. Second, the members of the Institute were obliged to request a letter of confirmation. Third, among the working rules for an audit report, all Corporate Accounting Standards, which had formed the criteria for decision at the expression of opinions in the financial statements, were deleted and replaced by so-called Generally Accepted Accounting Principles.

The establishment of the Japan Institute of Certified Public Accountants as the body responsible for setting the auditing standards has placed a huge burden on that Institute. Thus, the future developments of the Institute will be closely monitored. I would like to add that in Japan the Generally Accepted Accounting Principles have never been considered as a coherent system. Owing to this historical fact, the duties of the Institute became even more important.

As for the obligation to request a letter of confirmation described in the second point, I believe that they have learned from the practice in America that the auditor is obliged to request a management Representation Letter from the client company, in accordance with SAS No. 19 set forth in September 1977 by AICPA. According to 09 on page 119 of the *GAAS Guide 1992* (published by Harcourt Brace Jovanovich, Inc.), a management Representation Letter certifies that, among other matters, the book and records are correct and complete to the best of management's knowledge and belief, and there are no undisclosed or contingent liabilities (OBSERVATION 1).

In the United States, if the manager signs a false Management Representation Letter stiff penalty rules, including the Foreign Corrupt Practices Act, are applied. Section 7206 of the Internal Revenue Code, for instance, stipulates that those who make false entries can be sentenced to a maximum of three years of penal servitude or fined a maximum of $500,000, or both. If Japan's Ministry of Finance is earnestly committed to preventing false entries under Article 498.1.19 of the existing Commercial Law, then it should seriously amend this law in accordance with U.S. law provisions, rather than impose an ambiguous civil penalty of ¥1 million or less. Thus, it is inevitable that such Japanese laws, which lack transparency, are criticized by the U.S. government as an obstacle to a sound free-trade system.

In the request for a letter of confirmation, the items that need to be confirmed according to SAS No. 19 include the ordinary conditions of twenty items (A to T). Meanwhile, the Japanese letter of confirmation merely requires "at least" three items to be confirmed, namely that (1) management is responsible for preparing the financial statements, (2) all materials required to perform the audit are presented to the auditor, and (3) important contingent and subsequent events. It can only be said that the citing of these three conditions lacks candidness and is inconsiderate. For instance, paragraph (d) of SAS No. 19 provides for "absence of errors in the financial statements and unrecorded transactions." Paragraph (m) requests the declaration of whether or not there exist any "losses from sales commitments," while paragraph (o) requests the declaration of whether or not there exist any "agreements to repurchase assets previously sold."

In Germany, the German Institute of Certified Public Accountants decided that it was necessary to request a *Vollständigkeitserklärung* (declaration of completeness) from the client and thus put this into practice in 1936, forty-one years earlier than the United States. Japan, on the other hand, only undertook similar steps a full fifty-five years after Germany. To advance to the level of other countries, Japan must learn the lessons contained in *GOB*, written by Professor Leffson of Munster University.

As mentioned above, the third point called for abandoning the Corporate Accounting Standards and adopting the Generally Accepted Accounting Principles. This change stemmed from the collapse of the carte blanche theory concerning the principles of regular bookkeeping of the late Kotaro Tanaka, dean of the Faculty of law of the former Tokyo Imperial University. This was a natural development. Dr. Tanaka claimed that the principles of regular bookkeeping of the German Commercial Code have no substance and that the government has no way to insure sound accounting practices of private companies other than by the rule of law. One of the salient features of the Japanese academic circle is that this theory lives on as "provision of Taking into Consideration the Fair Accounting Practices" in Article 32 of the existing Japanese Commercial Code. This provision was prepared under the absurd theory that claims that specific accounting standards do not exist and only fair accounting practices exist. This provision will some day be revised because the general situation of the world will not approve of this view.

2. Revision of Certified Public Accountant Examination System in Japan

Japan's Certified Public Accountant Law was enacted in 1948 under the auspices of GHQ, commanded by General MacArthur. Thus the law has been in existence for forty-four years. Today there are roughly nine thousand certified public accountants (CPAs) in Japan. This means that on average approximately two hundred pass the CPA examination every year. I presume that Japan's Ministry of Finance has raised the specter of a shortage of CPAs amid the recent process of internationalization and diversification of the economy. Consequently, I believe, the Ministry plans to revise the law for the purpose of increasing the number of CPAs. It intends to accomplish this without lowering their professional level.

Japan's CPA examination is comprised of three levels: the first, second, and third examinations. The second examination constitutes the centerpiece of the examination process and is generally taken by college graduates. The proposed revisions call for amending this second examination, and have two salient features. First, the essay exam will be divided into two parts, a short-answer exam and an essay exam. Under the revisions, only those who pass the short-answer exam would be able to take the essay exam. Second, the old exam covered accounting, which includes bookkeeping, financial statements, cost accounting, and auditing theory. It also covered commercial law, economics, and management. The revisions call for adding civil law and allowing examinees to choose two of three subjects of economics, management, and civil law. In addition, there will be the compulsory subjects of accounting and commercial law. There are other minor revisions, which I will not discuss here.

Article 41 of the Constitution of Japan stipulates that the Diet shall be the sole law-making organ of the state. What worries me most is the fact that in reality Diet members are satisfied with simply expressing their approval or disapproval of a bill. In effect, Diet members do not actually draft bills. Nearly all bills are drawn up by government officials. This means that almost all Japanese laws are bound by the general disposition and the level of intelligence of government officials. More often than not, the general disposition of government officials is to defend their own interests and seek advancement, which has a tendency to produce laws that lack both foresight and courage. The intelligence level of Japanese bureaucrats is remarkably lacking in a viewpoint for examining various phenomena in a global perspective with the methodology of comparative laws. The world-famous superiority of Japanese bureaucrats is therefore limited by these factors.

In my opinion, the revisions of Japan's CPA examination system will augment the yearly increase of CPAs by a meager 20 percent, or less than fifty accountants a year. The revised law is in effect as of October 1, 1994. This means that the number of CPAs will grow by less than five hundred persons over the next ten years. In consideration of the recent global trend wherein an increasing number of corporations are having to disclose their financial accounts, this increase is paltry at best.

Britain, which has a population of 57.1 million, has upwards of 100,000 CPAs, while the United States, which has a population of 253.6 million, has over 300,000. Japan, on the other hand, has a population of 123.61 million but only 9,000 CPAs. This clearly indicates that the number of CPAs in Japan is abnormally small in comparison with its population. This dearth is made even more apparent when one considers the fact that there are, according to the Ministry of Justice, at least 25,000 large limited companies with capital of ¥100 million ($800,000) or more in Japan. (Source: Ministry of Justice in 1992).

Twelve EC countries unanimously approved the Fourth Council Directive of 25 July 1978. Article 51 of the Directive requires all large limited companies to be audited by auditors recognized by national law. This is the general trend in the civilized world, and Japan must be in step with it. To do so, in my opinion, Japan must rapidly increase the number of CPAs to around 30,000.

Index

Accounting: history of, 127–130; Japanese system of, 133–137, 155; standards, 137–138; "truth, fairness, and transparency," 140. *See also* Auditing; Bookkeeping
Adversity, attitudes toward, 119–121
Attachment, freedom from, 82
Auditing: human behavior, 140; intuition, 133; New Era, 130–133, 149–154; transcendental consciousness, 133

Barrier(s), 43, 48, 73
Behavior, 66; determined by inner impulse, 34, 50–51, 53; and study of auditing, 140
Bookkeeping, history of, 127–130. *See also* Accounting
Buddha(s), 58, 85, 99; asceticism of, 16, 108; living, 112; powers of, 83; search for True Self, 36, 39, 42; Ta-

thagata, 46, 114; teachings of, 68, 80–82, 86–87, 90–91, 97–112
Buddhism, 85, 88, 94; Chinese, 26, 81; five periods of, 80; Indian, 50, 82; Japanese esoteric, 26, 154; Mahayanist, 151–153; philosophy of, 50–51, 59, 64; Tendai, 80; Upanishadic school, 50, 53. *See also* Zen

Character, 52–54, 60. *See also* Schopenhauer, Arthur
Cognition, theories of, 41
Company employees: versus self-employed, 69–70; why they fail, 73–76
Concentration: "objectless," 53, 63, 125, 152–154; of the spirit, 98. *See also* Dhyāna
Confucius, 9, 12, 38; Confucianism, 105
Consciousness: annihilation of, 58; calculating, 146; cleansing of, 24–

Consciousness *(Continued)*
25, 52; egotistical, 121–122; inherited, 68; Krishna, 125; Pure, 59; self, 15; stream of, 85; surface, 79, 86; three-layered structure, 34, 50; transcendental, 61–63, 125, 133, 141, 146, 150–154; unification of, 8, 59

Death, 1, 27, 37–38, 100, 105–106, 114
Delusion, 14–16, 91; delusory thoughts, 18; most people deluded, 109–110
Descartes, Réne, 118–119, 151
Destiny, changing course of, 8, 54–57
Dhāraṇi, 26, 92. *See also* Meditation
Dharma, 51, 87
Dhyāna, 63, 88. *See also* Concentration; Meditation

Ego: absence of, 85; awareness of, 114; in business, 70–71; destruction of, 69–73; egoism, 15, 70; ego-pole, 133. *See also* Consciousness
Eliade, Mircea, 86
Employee(s): company, 73–76; four types, 73; self-employed, 69–70
Emptiness: essence of self, 56, 84–85, 90; experience of, 54–56, 58–60, 102; penetration of, 17–20, 51; purification of subjective/objective poles, 29, 51; Void, 20. *See also* Enlightenment; Self; True Self
Enlightened being, 46, 72, 120; powers of, 24–25, 52. *See also* Buddha; Enlightenment; Zen Masters
Enlightenment, 42, 44, 49, 51–52, 60, 81–82, 86–88, 94, 97, 100–102, 106–111; emancipation from "residual mental habits," 36; escape from cycle of life and death, 114; goal of Zen, 17–20; lateral thinking, 15;

not difficult, 20, 97–98; reality versus idea, 17. *See also* Emptiness; Enlightened being; Nirvana
Epistemology, 56–58, 104

Faith, 91
Fate, ability to change, 58–60. *See also* Destiny
Fear(s), 107–110, 114
Form, 104; in flux, 105
Freud, Sigmund, 34, 50–51

Goethe, Johann Wolfgang von, 36–37

Hegel, Georg Wilhelm Friedrich, 72, 79, 82
Hinduism, 59
Hume, David, 41, 56, 58, 64, 104
Humility, ix-x, 8
Husserl, Edmund, 28, 63, 65, 132–133, 140, 146, 150, 152–153

Idea(s), as representations of reality, 41, 56. *See also* Cognition
Illusion, 37–40. *See also* True Self
Insight, 92; attaining, 76–90; Buddhist, 107; conditions for, 91. *See also* Intuition
Intuition: attainment of, 76–79; definitions of, 77–78; necessary for auditing, 79, 141

Kant, Immanuel, 41–42, 57–58, 64, 104, 133, 146, 150, 152–153
Keller, Helen, 120–121
Kenshō, 87, 97–98. *See also* Enlightenment
Keynes, Maynard, 114
Koan, 28, 43, 115; barrier, 73; Gateless Gate, 116–117; Mu, 43, 48

Life: and death, 100; highest way of, 25–27, 91–93; how best to live, 2,

10, 14–16, 31, 113–125; meaning
of, 1; only lived once, 1–2, 27, 37–
38, 49; purpose of, 15, 21, 32;
shortness of, 125
Love, 122; parental, 3–6

MacDonald, Ramsay, 113–114
Marx, Karl, 58
Meditation, 13, 17–18, 26, 67, 85, 88,
98, 110–112, 154; "just sitting,"
43; koan, 28, 43; no-mind, 36; no-
thought, 18–19; use of mantras, 25;
zazen, 105–106. *See also Dhārāni;*
Enlightenment; Training
Mind: clarity of, 20, 92, 98; construction of, 51; cultivation of, 93–95,
117; as emptiness, 58–59; essence
of, 42, 92, 98; freeing, 21; formless-
ness, 35–36, 40–41, 63, 109–110;
fundamentals of, 33–95; purity of,
8, 27, 69, 83; "no-mind," 46; objectless concentration of, 46, 63,
125, 152–154; penetrating, 41; "residual habits," 15, 36, 53, 59, 85,
90, 95; Supreme Mind technique,
26; transparency, 47; turning point,
36; unconscious, 34. *See also* Consciousness; Emptiness; Meditation;
No-mind; Nothingness; *Paribhāvana;* Self

Nirvana, 87, 110–111, 154; powers
of, 86; as true knowledge of life and
death, 37; Western ideas of, 152.
See also Enlightenment
No-mind, 36, 47. *See also* Enlight-
enment
Nothingness, 24, 44–45
No-thought, 44, 46–47, 83, 117

Oneness: of consciousness, 59; of human race, 55; of self and others, 70

Paribhāvana, 53–54, 59, 60, 85. *See
also* Mind
Perception: *noema* and *noesis,* 29, 63–
65
Polarity: in every act, 133, 139; subjective and objective, 28–29. *See
also* Perception
Power(s): intuitive, 92, 141; miraculous, 86; spiritual, 78; superhuman,
8, 25, 81, 83, 93–94; supernatural,
27, 87, 111. *See also* Nirvana
Pre-Voice, 56, 84, 115, 122

Reality, ultimate, 56

Schopenhauer, Arthur, 8, 37–39, 50–
51, 53, 60
Seeing: seeing the mountain, 117–119.
See also Kenshō
Self, 122; actualization, 61; consciousness of, 15; control, 115–117; destruction of, 71; discovery of, 73;
divided, 51; essence, 42, 54, 56;
false, 90; "Kill the Self," 119, 121–
123; original, 118, 151; and others,
15, 123–125; prevailing over, 49–
52; purifying subjective self, 27–30,
52; search for, 16, 40–44, 46–47;
as subject, 35. *See also* True Self
Success: "Do not resent success of others," 9–11
Sutra(s), 92, 100: *Āgama(s),* 80, 102–
105; on delusion, 14; Diamond, 49,
82, 98–99; Heart, 24, 25, 27, 109;
Lotus, 8, 80–81, 83; Weight of Parental Kindness, 11–14

Thing itself, the, 57
Training, 24, 37, 83, 85, 91–92, 94–
95, 98, 107, 111; essential during
youth, 16; no mind, 48–49; no
thought, 46; physical, 4–5; religious,

Training *(Continued)*
82, 106; at risk of life, 92, 112;
spiritual, 40; under Ueki Roshi, 17–
18, 20–21; way to greatness, 26. *See
also Dhārāni;* Meditation
Transparency, 47, 72, 94; in accounting, 140
True Self, 16, 81, 90, 109, 115, 118–
119; discovery of, 60, 62; empty,
56; knowledge of, 35, 117; oneness
of, 70; search for, 33–35, 39, 40–44

Ueki Roshi, 2, 13, 16, 37, 63, 83, 87,
109, 116; power of, 111; teachings
of, 17–32, 43, 48, 52, 91, 125
Ultimate Way: as enlightenment, 20;
not difficult, 20–22

Water, five principles of, 30

Way, the, 64; of Great Learning, 105
Weakness(es), overcoming, 3–8, 10

Yoga, 86, 110

Zen, 17–18, 20, 63–64, 72–73, 88,
98; Chinese, 97; ideal of life, 125;
no-thought, 46; search for True Self,
35, 42
Zen Masters: Bankei, 105; Bassui, 41,
87, 98; Chien-chih, 20; Dogen, 43;
Hakuin, ix, 8, 47–48, 52, 62, 71,
93, 98, 153–154; Kukai, 25–27,
92–93, 106; Myocho, 64; Saicho, 8;
Shido Bunan, 72, 119, 121–123;
Takuan, 29. *See also* Enlightened
being
Zen patriarchs: Hui-neng, 49, 78, 82,
97–99, 100–102